PARCHMENT WHISPERS

INDU KADAMBI

INDIA • SINGAPORE • MALAYSIA

ISBN 979-8-89233-600-0

Osmotic Divinity

A Dedication

In a realm where keys were absent, she unlocked the door to find the inner spirit. With a heart generously bestowed, she imparted the wisdom of the Spirit. Perceiving the Divine within every religion, she transcended confines to discover the Supreme.

To her child, she spoke of drops forming oceans, while unveiling the vast ocean within each drop. With humility and gratitude, this offering goes back to her, a reflection of the spiritual wealth she bestowed upon me.

To Padmaja Rajagopalan, my mother.

Contents

Foreword

Any attempt to translate and at times offer new interpretations of any work, especially poetry, from the language in which it was originally written is a daunting and daring task. And translation of hymns to the divine, in this case the divine offerings in verse by Andal to Lord Ranganatha, from ancient chaste Tamil with its own unique idioms, syntax and cadences into English, a language with European ancestry differing markedly from the Dravidian tongue, poses a greater challenge. Many occidental scholars and linguists have translated oriental works, in particular Indic novelists and poets from regional languages into English. Those who have read for example the translations of Sanskrit or Kannada or Bengali poets and authors into English or the translation of nature poets like Wordsworth or Keats or Shelly into an Indian language will affirm that the translation suffers in conveying the flavours and intensity of emotions of the original. They lose something of the essence which is indescribable.

And Hymns to the Supreme or temple deities present additional difficulties while embarking on merely translating them. Those of us who heard Andal's verses in our childhood while visiting Shri Vaishnavite Temples along with our parents can still hear them echoing resonantly in our inner beings. We never understood the meaning but like the Vedic chants, hymns in churches with the deep ringing of church bells or the early morning Azans from mosques they cast a spell on us and transport us to a mystical world beyond our comprehension.

But one day when we are fortunate to grasp the meaning of those chants and verses when we grow up, and when those incomprehensible words which we heard as children are invested with meaning, we discover to our unbounded joy that their beauty is enhanced manifold because of their profundity.

That said who can deny the immeasurable value of translations and fresh interpretations of the world's literature into the various languages of the world! Civilisations have flourished only through the winds of cross fertilisation of ideas and cultural currents blowing across continents and countries through the ages. The Rigveda says "Let noble ideas come to us from all directions."

In this context Indu's offering of a bouquet of Andal's verses is a laudable labour of love.

Andal the only female poet saint in the Sri Vaishnava tradition of Hinduism, belongs in a way to the Bhakti and Sufi movement of tenth and eleventh centuries and alongside the pantheon of Meera and Kabir.

In the Meera bhajans for example, similar to Andal's hymns, the emotions of dissolving into Krishna, the longing to be united with him and the choice of words and phrases for passionate love are similar and characterised by attributes where God is both a person and principle – both Saguna and Nirguna.

We also see this in the songs of Bauls, a group of wandering mystic minstrels comprising of mainly Vaishnava Hindus and

Sufi Muslims from West Bengal and East Bengal (now known as Bangladesh) whose folk poetry had a great influence on Rabindranath Tagore. Here's a Baul song, in Tagore's translation which expresses it:

> The man of my heart dwells inside me.
> Everywhere I behold, it's Him!
> In my every sight, in the sparkle of light
> Oh I can never lose Him-
> Here, there and everywhere,
> Wherever I turn, right in front is He!

And now compare one of Andal's verses as rendered by Indu with an imagery that has lyrical intensity of emotions for her beloved-

She whispers, "His lips are so red, and his shoulders are mighty. But, as you know, it's only with those compassionate eyes that He captivates willing souls."

She then plants the parrot on her left shoulder. "Keep whispering the name in my ear," she encourages. "I vow to win him someday."

With the hypnotic "Ranga, Ranga" resonating in her ears, she sifts through the daily offerings.

This longing for Him, this primeval urge to fuse into Him, or to His Beloved, which is both anthropomorphic and abstract, which has form and is also formless characterises all Bhakti poetry and suffuses all mystic poets including Tagore.

The believers and the non believers who can read these in English are both blessed. These invocations to Krishna or Ranganatha seep into the soul of the devout. And the philosopher uninitiated into the Bhakti cult will find joy in the lyrical beauty of verses made possible by Indu's translations which capture the essence of Saint Andal's verses elegantly and effectively.

– Capt G R Gopinath
Bangalore
31ˢᵗ March 2024

What's in a Name?

It begins with a question—an age-old inquiry that has reverberated through time:

"If He's the One with infinite names, how must I call Him?"

This profound query, born from the depths of genuine curiosity, has echoed in the ears of the village priest on countless occasions. Yet, his response remains steadfast, a reliable guide through the labyrinth of divine complexity.

"The Omnipotent is multifaceted."

Within these words, there resides an acknowledgment of the boundless attributes that collectively shape the essence of the divine. Creator, preserver, destroyer. Parent, child, guardian. Consort, friend, child. Rescuer, refuge giver, hero, and heroine—these are but a few facets of the Supreme's infinite roles, defying mortal tongues' capacity to articulate the ineffable.

"It is for this very reason," the priest continues, casting a thoughtful gaze, "He is known as…"

"…the One with No Name," the devotee concludes, a paradox adding a touch of cosmic irony to the sacred inquiry.

Amid this paradox, where the questioner grapples with the enigma, an intriguing revelation often emerges when one steps away from the cacophony of daily life.

The devotees, caught in contemplation, seek to grasp the essence of the divine through the lens of His boundless forms. Yet, He eludes conscious memory, an ethereal entity radiating with countless facets. Their yearning intensifies, and their questions persist.

"Why must infinitude be confined by human limits?" they inquire, grappling with the existential quandary of comprehending the splendor of the Divine.

The priest, attuned to the frustrations, and aspirations of the seekers, steps forward, offering clarity in the face of complexity.

"One of the Omnipotent strengths is inclusiveness. Envision this world as His grand playhouse, where each of us is an equal participant."

Intrigued, yet not entirely convinced, the seekers ponder the notion of matching their finite brilliance with the infinite.

The priest, sensing the need for simplicity amid the intricate tapestry of divinity, imparts a guiding principle.

"If you wish to be part of Him, address Him with the purest love, in its simplest form."

"Can we then name him as one of our own?" they inquire, contemplating the prospect of a personal connection with the ineffable.

The priest nods, granting approval. The villagers, seizing this sacred moment, embark on a journey of intimacy with the divine. They christen Him Ranganatha, the Lord of the Stage. With a familiarity born of love, they affectionately shorten it to Ranga, unaware that this earthly playhouse extends to the vast expanse of the cosmic stage.

It is within this nameless quest for understanding that the stage is set, beckoning readers to delve into the unfolding cosmic drama where the divine and the mundane converge in a dance of eternal significance.

Chapter 1

The Temple Priest

In the heart of Srivilliputhur, where the resonance of prayers meets the divine, lives a priest whose devotion extends far beyond the sacred walls. His connection with divinity intertwines with the rhythms of daily life, where he not only tends to the spiritual needs within the temple but also nurtures the earthly garden with profound care. Proficient in the intricacies of worship and rituals, he is not just a guardian of traditions but a sincere poet, his verses echoing the essence of heartfelt devotion.

The priest's adoration for Lord Vishnu is a seamless tapestry woven with threads of tradition, service, and rituals. Adorning a necklace of *Tulasi* beads, symbolic of the sacred basil, his every action is a material manifestation of his reverence for the One residing close to his beating heart. Whether immersed in the sanctum's sacred silence or toiling in the vibrant expanse of the divine garden, his devotion remains unwavering. Like how the rhythmic churning of a milk vessel produces the butter of divine ambrosia, his thoughts incessantly churn with the essence of Vishnu.

In the temple town, devotion knows no bounds, transcending the barriers of caste, creed, and gender. It permeates the very air, seeps into the soil, and dances in the fragrance of blooming flowers. The mysterious greatness, hinted at by these subtle manifestations, goes beyond the apparent, echoing the indefinable nature of the Supreme.

As the priest tends to the garden, he embodies the essence of a yogi, understanding that he plays a small yet integral role in the abundance bestowed upon the hamlet. To the people of the town, he is not just a man with a name; he is Vishnu Chitta, the one whose thoughts are solely and eternally fixated on Vishnu.

Each day, with the gentlest touch, he picks flowers, carefully collecting them in reed baskets. In his hands, these blossoms transform into garlands and decorations, offerings of utmost devotion in the sanctum sanctorum. The flowers, in their silent beauty, believe they exist to serve the Lord, viewing the priest as the weaver of their destiny.

Bhoo-Ma, the Earth Mother, senses the tender reverence in the priest's touch, acknowledging his voluntary stewardship. Filled with gratitude, she yearns to reciprocate his devotion with a gift worthy of his love for the Spirit.

One dawn, as golden streaks pierce the dark sky, Vishnu Chitta enters the garden, thinking he has found the most exquisite flowers for his dear Lord. Yet, amidst lotus flowers, and Tulasi leaves, he discovers a perfect creation—a radiant baby girl, cradled in the embrace of the Earth. Smiling beatifically, she reaches out to him, and in that moment, a paternal love awakens within him. Naming her Go-da, meaning 'gift from the Earth,' he prostrates in gratitude to Lord Vishnu.

A father is born!

As he holds her close, feeling the echoes of the divine name, he is oblivious to the long-term plan woven into her existence. Born to rule over the One her father worships, she listens to the vibrations of his love, already resonating in harmony with his thoughts of Vishnu.

Goda's World

Goda grows and basks in the love of her father. He passes on to her the spiritual knowledge of the Lord, his immeasurable love and devotion, and the divine pleasure of serving Him. Sharp in comprehension, she absorbs the knowledge of His valiant deeds, deciphers the complex scriptures, and even nurtures the garden like him. With each passing moment, her rich love of the Lord gets more profound.

Her world is the garden. Goda weaves signature offerings of flowers and greenery for her love. This Supreme Being with a thousand names, Krishna, Vishnu, and Govinda, are only a few ways of seeking Him. She calls herself Ranganayaki, a privilege she has ascribed to herself as his mistress.

Rows and rows of beautiful flowers, ferns, and scented herbs thrive in the garden stimulating all senses. Heady fragrances escape four walls, leaving trails of scents perfuming the town. No one requests maps or directions to the temple. Instead, the smell invariably acts as a navigator.

Goda watches her father go about the garden and temple as she grows. She joins him daily in this service with an equal measure of devotion. He's serious, but she's playful and confident in her love for the divine.

Each flower vies to be part of Goda's garland. She ardently creates varied garlands for Ranga's broad shoulders. Some let out this desire and hope with an intense fragrance, while others stand out in color, shape, or size.

"Pick me for the garland!" the flowers voicelessly entreat. Some others blush unseen. Despite questioning their worthiness to be part of the garland, some blooms faithfully wait until they fall to seed.

Tulasi never goes through this exercise. She's the holy basil used for several purposes, including flavoring the sacred water. She aids, abets, and acts as a partner in Goda's feminine wiles. As a result, she gets extra attention from Goda.

Goda's imagination is unfettered, and she plays with creativity. One day it's weaving a garland from jasmine; she may fashion a posy out of them. She may, on other days, weave a wreath of tuberose and scented geranium for the intense fragrance. When the ardent love for him overwhelms her, she creates floral festoons that span the entire periphery of the temple housing her Lord. She stitches mango leaves together to make valances at entry doors. She finds inspiration everywhere she looks.

There are days when the brilliant sun plays hide-and-seek with the blue cloud. She remembers the feeling of his shining eyes opening and closing.

The *Atasi*, or flax flowers, remind her of his blue complexion. Two full lotus petals on the pond represent his eyes, pregnant with love for her. Her creations are playful in their devotion. Yet each day, she weaves a tulasi garland without a miss. The single red lotus she puts in the middle of this garland is a mysterious message between her and Ranga, meant for them alone.

The dark green leaves of the *Tamaal* tree are reminiscent of his emerald hue. Finally, she quits her yearning and decides to do something for him.

"Today, we will create a *Poo-chendu*," she informs her parrot solemnly. Cocking its head, the parrot looks at her questioningly.

"It's for his amusement." She continues to thread the flowers for the posy. "He will play with a decorative, scented ball of flowers."

The parrot leaves her shoulder to perch on perfectly spherical fruits, and she lovingly picks them. Then, she enrobes and tucks them with flowers and herbs to create flower balls. Sometimes she adds a frill of ferns around and a long stem for him to grasp with perfect hands.

"This one here is purely for style, decorative purposes only," she informs the curious green mimicker.

There are those days when He comes in her dreams. He thanks her for the beautiful love-enhanced creations. Sometimes, they play games together. He will then tease her with a hint. When the blooms beckon brighter than the sun and the spiky scented flowers burst forth, she will interpret His wish.

People from distant corners come to behold the garlands of sunflowers (*Suryakanthi*) and Indian medlar (*Bakula*). She gives him the answer; her lover's the glorious sun, and she's the scented Myristica fragrans known as *Surabhi*.

One early morning, when the sun breaks with a golden flourish on the eastern sky, she gets another inspiration.

"Golden skies, and there's the request for the day," she announces to her girlfriends. They turn their heads to spy a profusion.

In the quiz of hints and signals, Goda deciphers His requests. When the sun breaks, she gathers golden-hued flowers in response to His request.

Her friends delight in her ability to interpret these mysterious dialogs. "*Kanakambara* flowers! He must have spoken about the golden sky today," they exclaim, unable to fathom how these flowers become even more glorious adorning His broad shoulders.

"Ah, the games we play," she mockingly sighs to the *Kadamba* flowers remembering the forest where she and her lover frolicked.

The dawn heralds brighter days as Goda concocts perfumes, generously giving them away. Her compassion shines through every action. The screw pine, perceived as lowly by some, receives attention, as she extracts its heavenly fragrance, creating sachets for the people in her town, demonstrating one more way to share nature's infinite abundance.

Now and then, she picks an imperfect flower or leaf to add to the glorious creations. Don't they want the opportunity to get closer to the divine? This combination of devotion and compassion makes her designs infinitely beautiful.

The coral stems of the creamy and fragrant *parijata* flower remind her of His lips on the white conch. She shivers slightly, sensing his breath upon her. Goda makes a chain of the blossoms and wears them close to her breast. It makes her restless, and she feels strangely afire. She makes herself a paste from the sandalwood to cool her ardor.

Back in the garden, the fragrant scent blend of champak, patchouli, and artemisia, wafts unendingly, and it's easy to become delirious if you stay too long. The night jasmine, continuing the scent festival, ensures that the fragrance lingers even when the water lilies bloom at night.

Unpicked flowers sag in defeat, and some optimists put out seeds hoping for the opportunity to serve in the garland in another life. On the other hand, the frangipani insists that it's the official temple tree with its heavily aromatic blossoms. The flowers shudder at such arrogance from the parent, and they voluntarily detach themselves to fall to the ground like stars on Earth.

Her Enchanting Ploy

Not far away, the emerald hills resemble His sculpted shoulders. Goda reminisces about the river Kaveri, gracefully winding its way around the abode of Ranganatha in Srirangam. Inspired, she conceives a plan to translate that image into a dedicated creation using Tulasi leaves. Just like that sacred river, her garland of green leaves will elegantly encircle the Lord's divine shoulders.

It's a cherished routine for Goda. She adorns herself with the garland, gazing at her reflection in the lily pond. After assessing its size and length, a satisfied smile graces her face. She twirls around, eliciting appreciative squawks from the parrots in the courtyard. The fragrance she imparts saturates the green leaves. Following her routine, she delicately removes the garland, fluffs it out, and places it carefully in a clean reed basket. Soon, her unsuspecting father will carry the "once-worn" garland to the Lord in the inner sanctum. As per tradition, he believes it to be a fresh, untouched offering for the adornment of the Lord.

Tulasi is aware of Goda's fervent pursuit of Narayana. The fragrant herb willingly aids and abets her, finding honor in being the medium that unites the Supreme Lord and Goda.

"Ranga, Ranga, Ranga!" murmur the parrots in the courtyard quadrangle. The coral-beaked one settles on Goda's palm. She needs him. Goda considers herself a flower in the infinite Bhakta Garden. She smoothens his feathers and whispers, "Who can resist the Brave One, and can we blame the adorers?"

The green one nods his head in agreement.

She whispers, "His lips are so red, and his shoulders are mighty. But, as you know, it's only with those compassionate eyes that He captivates willing souls."

She then plants the parrot on her left shoulder. "Keep whispering the name in my ear," she encourages. "I vow to win him someday."

With the hypnotic "Ranga, Ranga" resonating in her ears, she sifts through the daily offerings.

Caught in the Act

Some days, the flowers get rebellious.

Goda meticulously selects specific blossoms, challenging them to outshine themselves. Today, a cascade of blooms from shrubs that flower once every twelve years adorns the garden. It's as if the flowers are engaged in a friendly competition, with some doubling their usual size while others intensify color. The fragrance reaches its peak, intoxicating anyone within a few steps.

Amid this floral fervor, Goda walks through the garden. Her usual graceful gait falters, influenced by the heady atmosphere. Among the intoxicating scent of champak blossoms, reminiscent of her lover's allure, she tries on the Tulasi garland. Unsteady, she gazes at her reflection in the well.

"Goda, the Lord's garland is not in the basket," her father's concerned voice floats towards her. Snapped out of her reverie, she reassures him that it's on the way.

In her heightened state, Goda removes the garland meant for Him and places it in the basket. Unbeknownst to her, a long strand of her lustrous hair gets entwined in the floral festoon.

Unaware of her state and the once-worn garland, her father, reassured, takes the daily offering to the inner sanctum. Initially, he notices the leaves looking a bit flat, so he gently massages and fluffs them. Sensing a loose thread, he unravels a strand and is startled to see what appears to be a young maiden's hair.

Perplexed, he summons his daughter and questions her about this unexpected addition.

"I wore the garland around my neck, father."

Despite her innocence, he's mortified, as he tries to fathom this perceived blasphemy.

"Child, why would you commit such a grave act?"

Unaware of any wrongdoing in the name of love, Goda replies, "He's my husband, and that's why."

Her organic response sends shockwaves through him, leading to a rare moment of chastisement.

For the first time, he reprimands her. How could an ordinary mortal accept something meant first for the Lord? Only the Goddess Lakshmi, His consort, has that right.

"Out of love, dear father, I did it out of love, and that's all."

Overlooking her simplicity and clear eyes, the father is unable to calm his agitation.

Never having judged her harshly until now, he feels a sense of outrage at her action. Biting his tongue, he introspects on the serious error, realizing it is his fault. He offers a heartfelt apology to the Lord.

Surely the Lord must be insulted by the used garland. The priest discards it and fashions a virgin one with the freshest flora. Will the Lord forgive his grave oversight?

He places the resplendent garland on Ranganatha's mighty shoulders, only to see it descend to the ground like a slithering snake. Attempting again, the garland slips away once more. Worried and apologetic, he tries repeatedly, but each time, the garland falls, as if the Lord is rejecting the virgin offerings with disdain. Vishnu Chitta begins to feel he has committed a dereliction of duty.

Broken in spirit, he enters a repentant mode, offering to atone in any possible way for this perceived negligence.

The Realization

In the stillness of the night, Vishnu Chitta's heart weighs heavy with remorse. The revelation about Goda's longstanding practice of offering her once-worn garland over several years pierces through his soul like a relentless thorn. It wasn't a momentary lapse but a repeated oversight, and the gravity of this realization gnaws at him. As a priest, he has violated tradition. As the parent, he grapples with an enormous sense of guilt and failure, questioning himself for not being vigilant enough. Sleep eludes him as he contemplates the gravity of the mistake that has been unknowingly allowed to persist.

The dejected priest, seeking solace, turns his thoughts to the mighty Ranga, engaging in a trance-like meditation. In this vulnerable state, a voice, both gentle and powerful, cuts through the silence: "Why did you throw away MY garland?"

The question echoes, and the priest, initially bewildered, begins to fathom the depth of his unintentional transgression. The Lord's inquiry isn't about the rejection of new garlands; it's a lament for the absence of something more profound.

In the solitude of that sacred space, Vishnu Chitta is confronted with a divine truth that transcends rituals and traditions. The Lord, in a mysterious revelation, unveils His desire for the fragrance of Goda's love and devotion encapsulated in her once-worn garland. The priest stands dumbfounded, realizing that the simplicity of her offering holds a significance that surpasses his understanding.

Morning breaks, and Goda, untouched by the turmoil of the night, prepares herself with unwavering devotion. The Tulasi garland, a symbol of her love, delicately graces her neck. Strangely, her father, now touched by an invisible force, stumbles into the sanctum, carrying the once-worn garland. Anticipating rejection, he places it on the Lord, only to witness a miraculous acceptance that bathes the deity in unparalleled brilliance. In that moment, Vishnu Chitta's sorrow transforms into boundless joy, realizing that the Lord seeks the unadulterated love embedded in the offering.

Overwhelmed with understanding, he rushes to find Goda, who stands in the garden, a picture of serene devotion. With a radiant smile, she hands him a lotus, a gesture that speaks volumes. In that instant, he comprehends the essence of devotion—love that transcends rituals and rites. Goda, the embodiment of Lakshmi Devi, becomes Andal, The One who Ruled the Lord.

In a break from tradition, the elder surrenders blissfully at her young feet. Little did he know that this act of pure devotion would set a tradition for centuries to come, with the temple at Srivilliputhur continuing to offer the Lord the garland first worn by His eternal consort.

Chapter 2

The Great Enchanter

Her heart begins to beat like a drum, resonating with the distant roll of thunder as He draws nearer.

In her mind's eye, she envisions His splendor—a perfect being standing tall atop a rocky hill with steps hewn from stone. An out-of-body experience propels her to ascend those steps, her feet moving to a mysterious drumbeat. Climbing higher and higher, she anticipates the nearness to the inner sanctum, where He stands as a shining beacon. Each step quickens her sense of anticipation, and the awe-inspiring majesty seems to grow exponentially. Time and space fade into irrelevance.

Reaching the glowing inner sanctum, she feels like a tiny flame, a solitary oil lamp, while the Supreme radiates like the light of a trillion suns. Her surrender becomes a victory. He is a contradiction, a master magician. How does His heart glow intensely from the lights of infinite lamps? Why does that light, with the potential to scorch, soothe like sandal paste? Clinging to His lotus feet, she senses Him bending, and lifting until her little glow merges into His illumined heart. She is finally home! She yearns to share her urgency to unite with Him, but before she speaks, she hears His words.

"I cannot exist without you."

How is that possible? Yet, why is she not surprised? Is it because her once restless flame has merged with an inexplicable force?

"I wanted those words to be mine." She never utters these words, but He understands, nonetheless.

"There can be no mine or thine. Your devotion is my force. The universe is out of many, yet the Supreme is One."

Continuing with what feels like a gentle command, He says, "Go find them all; show them how to ignite the lamp within."

"Do they need to be taught? You are an extraordinary contradiction."

"Then start with something that makes sense, something familiar, and that something will lead them to me."

Searching for a clue, He hints with a glimmer of mischief, "The answer may be in your garden."

Andal's shuttered eyes flick open as if a switch from an unborn era has been turned.

The soft flames on the circle of oil lamps have diminished, and some have even gone out. With a strange resolve, she contemplates, "I must replace the old wicks and replenish the oil."

He has given her a mission, and those cryptic words echo in her mind. Did she imagine what He said?

"You are me, and I am you."

What did He mean by telling her to find them? To whom was He alluding?

Although forever in plain sight, why does it feel like a hide-and-seek game with Him?

With the Divine, everything sounds contradictory, and consistent at the same time. Therefore, there are many names, and forms for the One Enchanter. Otherwise, how could one understand such infinity?

Chapter 3

Planting the Seed

The priest has just finished services for the morning when the daughter comes to him for counsel.

"He articulated mysterious things. I must do something to piece it together, but I don't know what it is."

He looks at her with great attention.

"The Lord appeared in my dream."

He sits down on the stone porch. "What a blessing, dear child!"

"The answer he said, is in the garden. What did the Supreme mean by that, father?"

The elder does not answer. Perhaps it's his kind way of testing her. Is she ready to be a spiritual guide? Instead, he asks her what her role is in the garden.

"Father, I plant seeds; I depend upon the sun, soil, and water. Then, I take care of the garden. I then harvest the bounty for the giver and his people."

The father circles back to the beginning.

"Child, what did you say you do first?"

"Why father, I first plant seeds."

"Seed planting," the father articulates, "is an important job. The remarkable thing is that it looks insignificant. Yet, the tiny seed holds the potential of a tree and many generations of forests."

Furrowing her brow, she questions, "So many people plant seeds. Does He leave the same message in their dreams?"

The father knows she is different from the others, and he responds, "Look at it this way. The Gita is a garden. The Vedas and Upanishads are like mighty forests."

"You taught me all that, father; you were my Guru."

The father replies, "You imbibed the divine nectar of the scriptures, and now you truly are a versed devotee. Your deep knowledge and immeasurable devotion have earned the right to expose this essence to everyone."

"I feel ready, father!" she cries. "What sort of challenges will I encounter?"

"You will find yourself alone; not everyone is ready, even if you are," replies the kind father.

"It's understandable; we're simple cowherd girls. However, not everyone can comprehend the complexity, father."

He nods in assent and says, "Our scriptures are considered esoteric. Many people find them too mysterious, forsaking the simple and essential spiritual truths they contain."

Even those who claim to be experts come up short at times. Such is the complexity of the simple truth nestled in the scriptures.

"The forest always looks dense compared to the seed, father."

Questions swirl in her mind. She knows she's different from the others, including her friends. To clarify her thoughts, she continues. "My friends are young, and they have their lives to live. Can they renounce it all in the quest for the Omnipotent?"

"The Lord recognizes human attachments and bonds. The understanding of Dharma is the most important of all. There will be time for everything; familial bonds, interest in material pursuits, and the ability to love in all forms. We carry within us the love for parents, family, soul mates, friends, and children. These experiences fall within samsara or the cycle of life."

She nods in assent, "And at all times in this journey, it's important to be firm in believing in the Supreme."

The priest brings back an awareness. "You were born with this understanding, and the trappings of samsara strictly do not affect you."

"What of the others?" She wants to know why it is different for them.

"Child, most people are like aimless wanderers."

She reflects on this point, and the father continues that people can be at different points in the quest for the Divine. Sometimes they need help.

"It's as if they need someone to dispel darkness to uncover the light."

"Gu-Ru," she utters in understanding.

The first verse from the Advayataraka Upanishad makes sense to her. She understands that the "Gu" syllable means darkness, and "Ru" means the dispeller.

"A guru," the father explains, "is a self-illumined guide. A guru has realized the Supreme and has no intent or desire other than to share this knowledge.

There are several gurus from several far-flung places, and they may lead you through varied rivers. Everything ultimately flows into the ocean."

"Dear child, you're ready, I can tell. You truly understand the power in all its simplicity and complexity."

With a slight hesitation, she replies, "They were all men, the Alwars, or Gurus I learned from, but I'm only a young lass."

As a response to her question, the father rekindles her memory of the day he observed a specific interaction she once had with friends

It was a sunny day, and Andal was engaged in the beauteous garden. Her girlfriends came over to pry her away from the verdant garden to go to the market instead.

"We'll have beads and colorful baubles," one friend had cried.

Not wanting to disappoint them, she made a compromise before stepping out to town.

"I'd like us to play a game. First, let's observe the different leaves on plants. Tell me what you see."

The girls agreed, and they began discerning beyond the green. There were yellow greens, gray-green, and blue-green in endless shades and hues. Some were variegated, while others were glossy and juicy.

"I had never seen a leaf like this!" exclaimed one.

"Look at the shape; are they all the same?"

The girls began their pursuit. Some leaves were long, some short, some like needles, and some like ellipses. Some were round; others were triangle-shaped.

"That leaf looks like a fan. I'd fan my loved one," remarked one.

"This one looks like a palm, and this is like a heart."

They saw them all, those in perfect symmetry, and asymmetrical others. They saw smooth and jagged edges, and each leaf had distinct venations ranging from soft to striped to branches. Leaves had textures, smells, and sizes. Some even tasted good.

They went about picking several leaves and comparing them. Then, finally, Andal reminded her friends about the market visit they had planned, and the girls realized that the beauty, colors, sights, and smells they sought were right under their noses.

"Let's play the flower observation game instead," cried one.

"I feel an acute sense of consciousness, and I will never look at the garden as I did until today."

The girls nodded vigorously in assent to the friend's observation and even wanted to go on a flower quest.

Andal remembered it was important to keep her promise, so she and her friends left the garden to go to town.

It was an exciting visit, but the awe she saw her friends display in the garden was lacking at the market.

Just for a moment, they had all paused to see something grand in the simple things often taken for granted. The poet's words awakened the mindset of seeing the extraordinary in objects under their noses.

Back to the present, the father segues into how we often weave stories of the mighty Narayana in the form of little Krishna to simultaneously understand the accessibility and immense majesty of the Supreme.

"He was a young boy who ate mud from the garden. When his angry mother Yashoda reprimanded and ordered him to open his mouth, Krishna mischievously refused.

"Did she succeed?"

Nodding his head, the father continues, "Do you remember what the mother saw in the young lad's mouth?"

Goda closes her eyes, transported back to that enchanting moment, and vividly reimagines the scene. In this captivating episode, Krishna's mischievous play leads to his mother's persistent attempts to inspect his mouth.

Finally, with a mixture of curiosity and determination, Krishna's mother succeeds in getting her son to open his mouth. An air of anticipation surrounds her, expecting to find mere mud that she would lovingly remove from his playful escapade.

Yet, what unfolds defies the ordinary and catapults the moment into the realm of wonder. Within that tiny mouth lies not just mud but the entire cosmos—the earth, the universe, and the planetary system. Krishna's mother finds herself beholding the macrocosm and microcosm simultaneously. Her own face becomes a reflection in the cosmic expanse contained within his baby mouth infinite and innocent at the same time.

The sheer vastness and intricacy of the universe contained in that small space send shivers down her spine. The Omnipotent reveals itself in the form of a naughty child, unraveling a simple truth through the lens of the extraordinary.

"Go with what they know, use what's familiar to their world, and follow what their elders have taught them. It's often the simple things that are most difficult to comprehend. Be their walking stick to help guide them to higher realms," the father assures his pensive daughter.

In this awe-inspiring revelation, the ordinary transforms into the extraordinary, and the simplicity of the familiar becomes a pathway to the profound. The father's guidance echoes the wisdom of recognizing the divine in the everyday, urging Andal to be a guiding presence for those seeking higher realms amidst the simplicity of life.

She interjects suddenly, "The seeds, father, I start with the seeds!"

"The seeds are enough, child."

"From there, they will understand the plant, a garden, or even the forest on their own."

His kind eyes tear up, and the proud father gives his blessing.

"Plant seeds, enkindle the lamp of spirituality. Now go forth and become that guide, that Guru. You are ready."

Chapter 4

Exploration

Monsoon rains douse the earth, raising the most delicious petrichor on this day sometime in the tenth century. The moist red earth resembles a young maiden's decorated hands. The temple pond, replenished with rain, looks still as a shiny mirror. Andal and her girlfriends decide to swim in it. While their young minds flit and flutter like butterfly wings, her mind, in contrast, is firmly on task. How will she spark the divine consciousness in the earthly realm? She watches some of the friends standing at the edges of the pool. Not all of them want to get in. A friend cautiously tests the temperature and depth with her little henna-patterned foot. Some sit around the pond banks, watching. Finally, to her surprise, one enthusiastic friend jumps in and finds herself deeper into it than expected. "The waters may look still on top, but they run deep," she gasps. A couple of friends hold hands and carefully, step by step, go into deeper waters. Then, one by one, they enter the pond and play. Finally, the girls call out to the others sitting out to join them. "Let's start with the surface and slowly go deeper," informs a helpful one. Slowly, the reluctant ones join in and begin splashing on each other.

Yes, we must start at the surface, understand something apparent, and only then should we go deeper into the unknown," articulates Andal as she walks closer to the refreshing waters.

She seamlessly incorporates the resourceful guru's mindset. "Here's my world before me, and my path starts by respecting familiarity."

The girls continue to frolic until the sun starts to dip. Then, in the orange dusk, they hurry home before getting caught in the dust kicked up by the returning cows.

Chapter 5

On Her Own

As night falls and the soft glow fills her room, Andal continues to string her thoughts, emphasizing the importance of starting small and building on what her young maiden friends already know. She envisions them as little seeds that will someday grow into mothers, and she aims to ignite the spark of divinity in them. Her eyes rest on the Siruparai, a tiny drum in the quiet corner, which senses a subtle transformation in the air.

Andal, contemplating the journey into the abstract, acknowledges the power of the drum. The drum, often overlooked, resonates with anticipation, ready to play a crucial role in this endeavor. There are several kinds of drums ranging from small to gigantic. These have specific purposes ranging from arts, communication, celebration, war, birth, and death to name a few. The word *Parai* references not just the drum, but also hints at an entity unlike any other.

"I must use a transforming yet transformational object," Andal muses, "I must learn from my unasked and unanswered word." Her gaze settles on the drum, and it seems to read her mind. "The leitmotif!" she exclaims, as the drum embraces its role, planning to transform itself in myriad ways.

In their mutual understanding, Andal envisions the drum as the object of pleasure, knocking at the mind's door with rhythmic beats, speaking of divine glory. The drum eagerly agrees to create a celebratory mood as the journey unfolds, promising to always beat the divine name.

Andal articulates her vision, mentioning the multifaceted meanings of *"Parai,"* and the drum feels a surge of purpose as poems begin to spring forth in Andal's mind. It anticipates being woven into the divine garland, incorporating the voices of damsels in the spiritual quest.

"Why does the poet feel compelled to share this divine sensibility?" the drum wonders, recognizing the potential role of a sincere teacher in awakening others. Andal, planting big ideas with tiny seeds, creates verses effortlessly, and the drum eagerly awaits each new day, ready to resonate with the spiritual journey ahead. "One verse per day is one more flower for the garland," Andal proclaims, infusing the drum with a sense of purpose as they embark on this transformative journey together.

As Andal envisions the theme of the first verse—prosperity— the drumbeats align with the awakening of the girls. There is clarity in Andal's quest, and the drum is ready to echo that clarity to the world.

In a moment of introspection, the drum feels grateful to be chosen. "My good fortune rests in a two-word question," the little drum ponders aloud, "Why me?"

The little drum begins to feel a sense of pride and humility, realizing it is part of something more significant. As Andal whispers, "Stay close," the drum understands that it is not merely an instrument but a companion on this profound journey.

"Why does the poet feel compelled to share this divine sensibility?"

The drum continues to ponder. Perhaps it is because not all of us have awakened one. Will she be the sincere teacher to put the girls on the path of divinity?

As Andal plants big ideas with tiny seeds, creating verses more effortlessly than a florist weaving a garland, the drum feels excited to beat out her messages with grateful enthusiasm.

Her energy imbues a sense of purpose in the vibrating medium. "Today, I am the willing little handheld drum, embarking on the first day with a brand-new verse."

The little drum whispers the first words with awe. The tight parchment records, reverberates, and resonates with the poet's energy.

Even amidst its kin of drums, the *Siruparai*, the little drum, finds strength in its beats and the divine fragrance of Andal. Clutching onto her, the drum eagerly anticipates the steps of each new day, ready to resonate with the spiritual journey that lies ahead.

Kinds of Drums

Temples house devotional drums. Celebrations like birth, marriage, festivals, and other happy events have specific drums and drumbeats. Funerals use drums as well. Drums convey news, alert people, and serve as an accompaniment to dancers. Some drums have beating sticks. Some kinds have straps that sit on the drummer's shoulders. Some big drums stand alone, and their largeness can accommodate dancers on top. There are several forms of drumbeats, and each one has its significance. Which drum will she choose? Is she going to stick to one or several kinds? Her heart tells her to start small at first, so the handheld *parai* is a fine choice. It will fit nicely in her plan. Relieved by the first baby step, she looks at the small celebratory drum.

A Celebratory Tradition, the Pavai Nonbu

Could there be a celebration on the horizon? It is an opportune moment for the bridal vow or Pavai Nonbu about to start in only a couple of days. It's timely that the girls will soon observe a vow through the *Dhanur* month for 30 days. This vow is to secure a good harvest for all and a suitable husband for themselves. This ritual is called the Pavai Nonbu, where the young maidens appeal to the Divine with a pure mind, body, and spirit. But, first, they offer prayers to the Goddess Kathyayini. Andal realizes she has twin goals in one. In the journey of spirituality with the devotees, she will also become a bride to the Lord. He will be her *Upayam* and *Upeyam*, her means, and her end in Himself. In her mad love for Him, she sees the Goddess, and the entire pantheon of Gods and Goddesses in Him, the Omnipotent! This spirit has over a thousand names, and she sees Him as her consort. Yet, the Supreme is the One, and anyone can have any number of ways, names, optics, and narratives to complement that glory. She will lead the girls in the path of Dharma and secure the gifts of the Lord. In this journey, the girls will discover that devotion is the gift from and the gift for the Divine.

The spiritually aware may not always depend on religion, rites, or rituals. Devotion or Bhakti is often organic, simple, and straightforward. These evolved individuals needed no gurus or teachers, but they served as examples of another way of reaching the Divine through pure devotion. However, most of us need a spiritual alarm to wake up.

A ritual brings kinship, camaraderie, and a common purpose to the social animals called humans. Understanding the microcosm helps as a starting point. The journey into the unfamiliar is not easy, but when it starts from a familiar position, it gradually leads to fulfilling depths unknown. It's a tradition in the hamlet to worship the goddess for ideal husbands. That concrete realm will be the launching pad to expose the splendorous majesty of the abstract one. The theme of the first verse is prosperity, as manifested to everyone. They will beat the drum, and the girls will awaken. There is clarity in Andal's quest. She understands that the curtain must be parted slowly to reveal the higher, sweeter, and divine plane.

Chapter 6

The Damsels and Their Vow

The enchanting glow of the full moon bathes the aromatic gardens in its silvery luminescence. Lost in contemplation, she gazes at the alabaster orb with eyes half-open, an indescribable excitement coursing through her. Even in the recesses of her consciousness, her dark-skinned love radiates with eyes so brilliant they seem to burn. Restless and seized by inexplicable feelings, she senses a fire behind the inky black sky.

It is Dhanur Masa in Vrindavan, or the month of Margazhi, as known in her southern hamlet of Srivilliputhur. Tradition dictates that throughout this month, the girls perform a sacred vow to attract an ideal life partner.

As dawn paints the dark sky with orange streaks, she, akin to a liberated mare, rushes to awaken her friends. However, finding them still immersed in the embrace of slumber, she is compelled to pull back.

Quickly recovering from her initial chagrin, she assesses their unpreparedness. The young maidens lie in languid repose, adorned in yesterday's finery, and ornaments. It becomes apparent that priming them for a more profound realm will be an uphill task.

Spiritually awakened beyond her years, she keenly feels the need to share this divine gift. Yet, before she can bestow this knowledge, she must first awaken those who slumber.

Awakening someone is no simple feat; sleep can be mental, physical, or even spiritual. While spiritual books, epics, discourses, and treatises abound, at this juncture, the Vedas, Upanishads, and Puranas wield no power over spiritual lethargy. So, where does she commence to kindle the essential awareness of a higher force?

How can she simplify to amplify?

The question of "Why must I do this?" never surfaces in her contemplation. Instead, an inexplicable force propels her, a profound desire to share—an imperative to gather, amplify, and unite with something more significant than the entire universe. This compelling pull, what she recognizes as the truth without veils, holds a magnetic power. Yet, she understands that for most beings, this journey is not as straightforward. Thus, she refrains from questioning the why and focuses on the how.

How can she engage and reach the scattered minds of young, unsophisticated maidens? The path must be made accessible, employing the familiar rituals, and allowing the girls to want to receive the sacred.

Understanding the Supreme is inherently simple; once known, everything becomes crystal clear. However, she must first lay the foundation of awareness.

In this hamlet, a specific rite marks the beginning of the Margazhi month. Young cowherd girls observe a vow to Goddess

Katyayani, expressing their desire to secure a partner akin to Lord Krishna. This tradition, echoing across centuries, is a ceremonial convention to elevate spiritual awareness—an initial step in the quest for the divine.

The poet conceives the idea of crafting a garland of verses, one for each day of the Dhanur/Margazhi month. Each poem aims to serve as a spiritual steppingstone, designed not just for the present moment or the young maidens alone but to resonate through centuries, offering a sense of permanence in an ever-changing world. Her intent is clear—to weave poems as keys unlocking spirituality in a world inundated with noise and glittering distractions.

In the illusion of material permanence, the material world challenges the goal. Mortals, bestowing titles of permanence on fleeting joys, are akin to children enthralled by the transient thrill of an amusement ride, believing earthly joys will endure. Like a willing cloth steeped in indigo dye, most are absorbed in the whims of the world, clinging to the undeserved permanence of material fantasies.

The poet, however, does not dismiss the material world with spiritual snobbery. Acknowledging its impermanence, she navigates within that framework, understanding that this too, is a reality in the briefest moment. She works with those entangled in the material world to lead them to a higher realm. While most traverse life in a way that is oblivious to the world beyond, everyone has access to the power of intuition—a sixth sense tapped by listening with the heart, not just the ear.

There are parallels with the great mathematician Srinivasa Ramanujan, attributing his rare insights to divine grace. In the waking state of consciousness, humans employ only five senses, proceeding step by step. However, incorporating the sixth sense allows one to soar through issues unbound by time or space. The challenge lies in shedding intrusive thoughts, fostering acute awareness of the present, and letting intuition play a significant role in decisions. Intuition is like Graham's number; it is difficult to conceptualize the infinite bits of information from unexplored layers of consciousness. Trusting intuition leads to safety, better decision-making, and self-preservation, connecting one to the protective divine.

The fortunate experience a transformative moment when the mortal becomes the seeker, inserting the quest in the question. Awareness of the temporary nature of once-perceived permanence becomes a catalyst for disengagement, and the search for permanence becomes both the journey and destination.

Observing with a sense beyond the traditional five is rare, yet layers of illusion make it challenging to discern truth from illusion. The simple and elegant truth becomes obscured over centuries as mortals adeptly weave incredible illusions. The mirage, though undeserving, wields significant influence.

Youth and beauty, health, and passion, money, and contentment—all are impermanent. The realization dawns with age, yet mortals fight over artificial constructs with ego and misplaced passions. Despite the inevitable departure from material possessions, greed, and ego persist until the last breath.

Chasing material gain without contentment is likened to Sisyphus rolling a boulder up a mountain eternally, a story of infinite longing in this life. The truth is plain to see but remains concealed beneath the warp of the material world and the weft of impermanence.

The poet comprehends how most people perceive the world and endeavors to work within that framework. She seeks to part the curtain of illusion by wiping off the dust from the soul mirror. The first step is awareness of the Supreme, leading to the fundamental question—Who is the One?

Gaining access to divinity is neither exclusively hard nor easy; the path cannot be a one-way street. In the Gita, Krishna declares, "Whether you give me a leaf or water with devotion, I will partake in it." Divine access is as simple as offering anything with love.

Chapter 7

Morning Allegory: The Weight of Love

In the serene hush of morning, she lingers by the doors, stirring the maidens from their slumber with tales of the Supreme drawn from the vast expanse of epics.

Her narrative unfolds with the divine dance of Krishna, entwined in the delicate embrace of his consorts, Rukmini, and Satyabhama. The subtle dance of love begins.

Satyabhama, a portrait of possessiveness, contrasts sharply with Rukmini, who understands the alchemy of love's multiplication when shared selflessly.

Enter Narada, the playful sage, orchestrating a cosmic symphony. He deftly weaves a challenge, baiting Satyabhama's ego. The dare is clear – publicly prove the depth of love for Krishna and the world in a *Tulabhara*, a delicate equilibrium of love on a scale.

Satyabhama, draped in opulence, confidently embarks on proving her love through material abundance. Precious gems, golden artifacts, and beguiling jewelry cascade onto the scale. Yet, the cosmic balance remains unmoved.

Undeterred, she exhausts her entire treasury – a cascade of gold, silver, and deeds to vast lands – all futile against Krishna's weight.

In the face of defeat, Satyabhama, humbled, and stripped of pride, seeks aid from her perceived rival, the modest yet devoted Rukmini.

For the first time, an awakening stirs Satyabhama. Could life be more than possessiveness and material wealth?

Rukmini, embodying selfless love, sets aside Satyabhama's material opulence. Instead, with utmost sincerity, she places a humble holy basil leaf on the scale. Instantly, the scale tips, burdened by the weight of her devotion.

This parable unveils the transience of ego in love, affirming that material possessions are but feeble metrics for devotion. Rukmini's humble leaf outvalues Satyabhama's golden treasures.

Captivated by the enchanting tale, the young maidens beseech for more wisdom on this profound love.

The storyteller obliges, guiding them to an illustrious friendship, one between Krishna, and his bosom friend Sudhama, steeped in the tapestry of selfless love.

Krishna's visit to Sudhama's humble abode initiates an exchange of love. Sudhama, with scanty offerings of beaten rice, fears his meager gift might disrespect the Lord of Plenty.

Krishna, savoring each morsel, unveils the transformative power of pure love. Sudhama's simple act transfigures his family's destitution into opulence and grandeur.

This single-minded love delights Krishna who is accustomed to opulent feasts devoid of such pure devotion.

Thus, the facets of Bhakti — true, pure, and unselfish — unfurl, paving a direct path to the Supreme. Through devotion, one transcends into a realm larger and more profound than mere existence.

The morning tableau concludes, leaving the maidens enraptured, their hearts resonating with the echoes of love's weight and its enduring significance.

Chapter 8

Interest Piqued

Intrigued by these captivating narratives, the girls' curiosity now extends beyond the confines of the tale, she observes.

"What is this *Bhakti* or divine love?" inquires one, her voice a melody of genuine interest.

"Can we also love like that?" echoes another, a symphony of hope resonating in her words.

The girls, seeking a connection between the forthcoming bridal vow and this elusive divine love, venture further into the realm of understanding.

"How can we obtain this divinity?" they pose a question that reverberates within her, signaling a thirst for spiritual enlightenment.

Unfurling the layers of wisdom, she imparts that unconditional devotion to the Supreme is not sufficient; one must also embody divine qualities. Recognition, practice, and adherence to dharmic principles become the steppingstones. This transformative journey demands the infusion of spiritual thirst into daily life, a delicate balance that she, as a teacher, must master to guide those receptive to such profound ideals.

She shares the simplicity of understanding the Supreme.

"Wake up early to concentrate your minds upon His form," she advises.

The eager girls, yearning for clarity, inquire about comprehending this divine form.

"We are all part of the Supreme, so concentrate on the creations to understand," she gently responds.

Their curiosity persists, and they seek more profound insights.

"Does 'all' include us too?"

With a nod of affirmation, the poet assures, "Not only our forms, but this connection embraces all sentient beings. From the smallest seed to the grandest tree, every entity, big, or small, contributes. Just as millions of droplets comprise the ocean, every being plays a part."

As the distant rumble of thunder and the electrifying streaks of lightning paint the dark sky, she directs their contemplation towards the Supreme.

"The small seed and the large tree," whispers one.

"The large trees and the forest," adds another.

The youngest girl, enchanted, claps her hands, exclaiming, "The seed!"

A profound hush descends upon the group, shifting from mere seeing to deep observation, fostering a profound sense of connection.

Recognizing the need to recharge their souls while igniting curiosity about the divine, the poet contemplates simplifying the journey into the abstract.

She introduces the word *'Parai,'* weaving associations that rest in the spiritual realm. Poems, like blossoming flowers, spring forth in her fertile mind. Each verse forms a link in the divine garland, incorporating the voices of maidens in their spiritual quest.

The theme of the first verse resonates with prosperity, manifested to all. With the drumbeats, the girls awaken, guided by Andal's clarity of purpose. The journey unfolds as they slowly part the curtain, revealing the higher, sweeter, divine plane.

Chapter 9

The Verses, One for the Day

The Speaking Drum

In the hushed moments before dawn unfurls her golden eye, I witness her ascent—the poet, my mistress of verses. Around us, her comrades are entranced in the seductive cadence of a sonorous spell. She enfolds me in the tender cradle of her arm, and in that sacred embrace, I become the vessel for her melodic articulation. Together, in rhythmic unison, the first *pasuram* is birthed—a lyrical offering, a poetic hymn to the Divine. A verse each day for the thirty days of the month, the *pasuram* is a sweet and meaningful pulse, designed to rouse those submerged in the depths of slumber. It is an ode that transcends the temporal, a whispered call to awaken the dormant souls to the divine.

As the drum, I echo with the pulse of Andal's verses, beating in the first person to narrate the segmented understanding of these thirty poetic compositions.

In the initial rhythm, I beat purposefully for the first five verses, encapsulating the intention to perform the bridal vow. Together, we pursue the astounding Narayana, envisioning Him through the lens of Krishna, the God of love. In this rhythmic tapestry, we navigate the ritualistic approaches and thread the path of dharmic dos and don'ts.

Moving to the next set of beats, spanning verses 6 to 15, I participate in a collective call to action. The infinite facets of the Supreme unfold through epic narratives, revealing themselves in the rhythm of the verses. We identify obstacles obstructing the alchemy of the spirit, accompanying the attempts to awaken the highest spirit within this group of young maidens.

As we transition to the third set of beats, encompassing verses 16 to 20, I too herald the awakening of the divine spirit. The beats resonate with the efforts of the maidens as they seek to awaken the dormant divinity within themselves and their surroundings.

In the fourth set of beats, echoing through verses 21 to 28, the beats become a part of the harmonious symphony of laudation and mirroring. We celebrate and reflect the grandeur of the Supreme, mirroring the devotion of the maidens as they extol the virtues of the Divine.

Finally, in the last segment, verses 29 to 30, my beats synchronize with the rhythm of spiritual actualization. This transformative rhythm marks the culmination of our poetic journey as the maidens realize their spiritual potential.

In my beats, I carry the melodic interpretation of Andal's verses, inviting you to dance to the rhythm of this profound exploration into the divine. Each segment, like a distinct beat, contributes to the symphony of spiritual revelation woven into these verses.

Chapter 10

Segment A

DAY 1

Margazhi Thingal

This month is called Margazhi.

The inaugural ode unfolds with a gentle reminder, my heart resonating with sincerity as I serve merely as a drum, the vessel for her poetic symphony. The verses, delicately rendered in italics, bear the weight of my humble translation, seeking forgiveness for any inadvertent errors, omissions, or liberties taken in interpreting her sacred words. I am confident that the poet discerns the essence of my intentions.

"On this propitious first day of Margazhi, prosperity unfurls its abundance in every corner. Awake, O maidens, draped in resplendent attire, and adorned with ornaments! Why linger in slumber when the universe beckons?"

She endeavors to rouse them, not merely from their physical repose, but from the dormancy of their consciousness. He, Narayana, stands at their threshold—the Enlightened One, the Supreme, the Nameless One despite infinite names and indefinable definitions. How does one embed the divine spirit within the soul? Spirituality is a journey, and not all are prepared. Rituals sometimes serve as scaffolds or walking sticks in the ascent.

In their microcosm, the damsels adhere to vows, seeking soulmates through marriage. The poet deftly weaves these commonplace rituals into the tapestry of divine connection. Addressing them as *"yem paavai,"* my young ladies, she underscores that the journey begins within their familiar world, a pilgrimage from the microcosm to the macrocosm—an invitation to all.

Her voice resonates with an enigmatic depth as she introduces the divine as Narayana. *"He's the fearless lion of Yashoda and the son of Nandagopa, tall, and dark-skinned, exuding authority with a sharp spear and an intense, red-eyed glance. His visage, a paradox of the brilliant sun and the compassionate moon."*

Understanding a contradiction is no facile task. The name Narayana, layered, and complex, challenges comprehension. Yet, she sparks curiosity about the great Narayana, bringing him into their conscious realm.

Awareness is not consciousness; she devises a routine in the initial verse to guide the seekers on the path of divine love. A tranquil river bath at dawn purifies the mind, body, and spirit, setting them on the sacred path.

"Let us bathe early in the river's embrace to attain the great Narayana."

He, elusive, and multifaceted, is a giver, a provider of shelter, and by himself, the loftiest goal. Yet, the Supreme resides within the hearts of beings, reaching out to the highest reality infusing daily life with myriad hues.

I take center stage to reverberate her thoughts.

"We must celebrate with the world, and the drum is our key. Only the divine spirit can bestow it upon us. Awake, young maidens!"

Her dark-skinned love favors this month, echoing Krishna's affirmation in the Bhagavad Gita. She conveys that he loves the Margashira month, a time when the earth yields abundant crops. The bright star *Mrugashira* gleams with the full moon, a time of prosperity neither hot nor cold. *Brahma Muhurtam* is that auspicious time aligning with the divine and the mortal—an expansive channel for spiritual practices.

Navigating the complexities of astrology, astronomy, divinity, and gratitude, she beckons the young lasses. Amidst the material abundance of the harvest, she leads them to their origin.

In a world tethered by time and space, where anchors hold firm, she composes the second verse for the second day.

DAY 2

Vayathu Vazhvirgal!

All Ye World Residents!

Her slender fingers beat the tautly stretched skin on my frame. I feel as if we are waking up the universe together. It is the second day of the quest. Setting our intention to get Lord

Narayana's attention, we listen to her poem. What do the words mean?

"Oh, young maidens of this world, let us join forces to follow these steps for conducting our vow. We are to obtain the Supreme. When we find Him, we will hold steadfast to his feet. He's far away, in deep slumber (regarding us), while resting on the plump coils of the infinite Adisesha. So let us not indulge in milk, ghee, and delicacies that keep us from reaching him. Ringing the eyes with kohl or enhancing physical beauty with fragrant flowers on self will not help pierce his inattention to us. He is impervious to superficiality. Our goal is to reach divinity by thinking good thoughts, doing charitable deeds, and not using hurtful words. We must keep in the path of Dharma, for this is the way of our vow."

The poet, with every beat, guides the journey into the depths of spiritual understanding, inviting readers to ponder the essence beyond the superficial trappings of life. Her words paint a canvas of introspection, urging individuals to consider the impact of their choices on the path to divinity. The quest for Narayana transcends the material world's allure, beckoning seekers to move beyond the superfluous. The metaphorical anchors of material indulgence and superficial adornments become apparent, prompting reflection on their role in tethering souls to the transitory.

The pursuit of divinity, the poet contends, requires a conscious shift—a departure from self-absorption toward an awareness of profound truths. Kindness, charity, and knowledge emerge as the cobblestones paving the path to the divine. In this intricate dance between the material and the spiritual, the poet challenges the notion of permanence attached to worldly pursuits.

She weaves her narrative through the complexities of spiritual evolution, invoking the symbolism of Adisesha—the mythical snake representing infinity. Questions about the nature of time, the endless cosmic journey, and the potential chapters of human life linger, encouraging contemplation about the interconnectedness of existence.

Through the exploration of Dharma, Andal elucidates a path that transcends the dichotomy of good and bad. The intellect emerges as a tool, guiding individuals to discern the profound from the illusory. Choices, the poet suggests, hold the power to shape destinies, emphasizing the importance of ethical conduct and service to others.

I am only a percussive instrument, yet I echo with the resonance of spiritual wisdom. The poet's words, steeped in metaphor, and allegory, elevate the narrative to a profound exploration of the self and its connection to the divine. With each beat, I become a conduit for transformative reflection, beckoning listeners to peel away the layers of illusion and discover the timeless truths beneath.

In this awakening journey, the poet's verses serve as a guide, urging readers to navigate the intricate dance between the finite and the infinite. As I beat in synchrony with the poet's words, the quest for Narayana unfolds—a quest that transcends the limitations of the material world and invites seekers to embark on a timeless exploration of the soul.

DAY 3

Ongiulagalantha

The Exalted Measurer of the World Sunlight paints the temple walls like radiant smiles on the faces of maidens gathered. As the dawn unveils its golden hues, a group of maidens attune their senses to a sacred verse. In harmony, their hearts resonate with sincerity, absorbing the profound words of a poem that transcends time. This verse, etched into the annals of existence, unfolds a narrative that weaves through the cosmic tapestry.

"The Omnipotent, in a divine play, once embodied the form of Vamana, a diminutive lad. His stature, though small, stretched infinitely, revealing the authenticity of his divine essence. He measured the three worlds with this celestial form. We, as humble damsels, reverently take His name, praising the boundless grandeur. Immersed in the divine appellation, let us cleanse our spirits and chant His sacred name.

In our fervent prayers, we beseech the universe to cast away the shadows of evil. With each plea, we invoke the manifestation of abundance through compassionate showers thrice a month. The fertile earth reciprocates, yielding quality grain from the lush, tall growth of paddy fields. This flourishing expanse becomes a playground for joyful fish, and vibrant flowers cradle bees in peaceful slumber. Overflowing pails of milk, willingly shared by the cows, stand as a testament to the inherent abundance. May this prosperity and verdant bounty extend eternally, benefiting all creatures in the vast expanse of the universe."

In the wake of these verses, a profound realization dawns – we are but players in the intricate web of life, holding the potential for significant expansion within the cosmic interplay.

This verse becomes a guiding melody, prompting a mindful attunement to the minutiae of each passing day. Delving into the intricacies, gratitude fills the heart, and an awareness of *interconnected reciprocity* emerges.

With the blessing of copious rain, life forms thrive, finding joy in replenished pools where fish play gleefully. Green vegetation becomes a source of sustenance for contented cows, reciprocating with generosity through engorged udders ready to fill pails with creamy milk. The willing cooperation of the cows, guided by the gentle words of the maidens, transforms the milking process into a seamless flow of kindness.

This generous world, sought by the maidens, extends beyond human, and cattle life forms, reaching a crescendo in the *Vaibhavam* – the majestic splendor, glory, and power that permeate the cosmos. Devotees, in celebrating this divine essence, elevate their own qualities through acts of kindness, gratitude, and reciprocity.

In profound realization, we acknowledge that we are not isolated islands but *interconnected* beings, each playing a unique role in the cosmic symphony. The diverse elements – leaves, twigs, fruits, buds, and bare bark – coexist, grow, and prosper together, bound by an inexplicable force.

The poet, with each carefully chosen word, plants the seed of *collective prosperity*. The vision of flourishing individually and together stirs a profound beauty within our souls. United, we recognize the power we hold to make a difference, a realization that energizes us as we embark on the journey of life.

"The Omnipotent once appeared as Vamana, a tiny lad, and he took on an infinite loftiness to show an authentic self. He measured the three worlds with this form. We, damsels, take His name to laud the limitless stature. Immersed in the name of the Highest One, let us bathe, and chant his name.

We pray for the universe to exist without evil. We request the abundance manifest itself in compassionate showers occurring thrice a month. Paddy's lush, tall growth in reciprocation will give out quality grain. This fertile growth creates a playground for fish to jump in and out, and the beautiful blooms of flowers cushion shining bees cocooned in peaceful slumber. Overflowing pails of milk from willing cows are proof of abundance. Let this prosperity and lush vegetation forever benefit all creatures in the universe."

Suddenly I see the entire world and the interdependent creatures in this web we call life. We assume minor roles in this cosmic interplay while holding the potential for significant expansion.

This verse makes me tune into the little moments through each day. First, I hone in on the small details, and my heart fills with gratitude. Then, I put these details together to see interconnectedness.

The *Vaibhavam*, or majestic splendor, the glory, and the power he wields permits accessibility. The devotees augment high qualities by celebrating with kindness, gratitude, and reciprocity.

We may be different, but our connection to each other is undeniable. We hold together and are held together by something inexplicable. If we perceive the ultimate reality as a tree, then the leaves, twigs, fruits, buds, and bare bark are all different, but they grow, and prosper together.

DAY 4

Aazhi Mazhai Kanna

The Giver of Copious Rain

I resonate, not merely as a passive medium, but as an instrument responding to the gentle strokes of my poet's delicate fingers. Her rhythmic strikes coax divine grace from the depths of her being. Although the Supreme remains unseen, she conjures awe-inspiring majesty through analogies and metaphors drawn from the world of damsels, a realm untouched by the concept of a higher power until now.

"O dear Lord, let the rain pour forth abundantly. Withhold not even a drop."

At this moment, the Supreme transforms into the Rainmaker, channeling torrents after drinking from the deep ocean. As we marvel, the poet unveils the larger-than-life quality inherent in a Supreme Being.

"Your proportions inspire awe, akin to the rain-laden dark sky. The glittering wheel or chakra in your hands manifests as lightning, and thunder becomes your Valampuri conch. O Padmanabha! Your divine bow Saranga releases arrow-like raindrops. We implore you

to dispatch them without delay, nourishing our world as we revel in the seasonal waters."

Through her words, the poet illuminates the divine magnificence. We, in our minuteness, are prompted to step beyond ourselves and marvel at the vastness of His universe.

The poet extends appeals for friends and self, using vivid descriptions to reveal the treasures of the world. Joyful bathing in *Margazhi* season pools gives way to contemplation of the wheels of time, seasons, and the breathtaking wonders of nature. Friends, now awakened, keenly observe their microcosm, and expand their prayers for rain to bless the entire world.

Through her eyes, I witness the awe-inspiring grandeur of the Lord in the dramatic landscape, quickening the pace of my beating heart. There's something higher to aspire for in the daily, a majestic journey beckoning. Yet, within this rhythmic frequency, a peculiar question vibrates – *can I expand into this majesty?*

Upon closer inspection, the representations emerge. There is a greater order of things, and leaning into this universe provides a sense of belonging, connection, support, and trust. The *Valampuri* conch, with its sinistral curl, a natural rarity, is associated with prosperity, and blessings, evoking positive vibrations when blown. Both the conch and chakra serve as metaphors, awakening, and expanding minds, embodied in the forms of thunder and lightning, while the arrows from the Saranga bow symbolize the outpouring of divine wisdom in the form of precipitating rain for receptive minds to claim.

DAY 5

Mayanai

About the Enchanter

In the early morn of the fifth day, a poignant scenario unfolds.

A young friend, in a sudden epiphany, grasps one facet of the Infinite, struck with awe, feeling suddenly incapable, and insignificant. The Supreme must be an illusionist or a master magician, too lofty for her likes.

Past errors taint her self-esteem, and she questions her worth in being part of the spiritual quest. Fears mushroom one after another, and everything seems insurmountable obstacles.

"I am a mere mortal."

Genuine seekers through time have undergone tests, trials, and tribulations, but how can I in this naive group of young cowherd girls face them?

From my corner, I witness Andal's keen attention. She weaves the fifth verse offering an appropriate, fear-alleviating response.

Her words form an aural garland offering.

"Here, the avatar is Lord Krishna of Mathura, the wondrous magician, an illusionist who alters the course of fate for the greater good. He is ever-present."

She conveys his accessibility and approachability with the metaphor of the child form of Krishna and pulls his common lineage with her.

"You may find him playing on the bank of the exalted Yamuna River at a given moment. He claims to be of cowherd lineage. He brightened the mother's womb as a divine lamp. The wondrous Lord is approachable as that child, yet kept in mind like mischievous Krishna, bound by a mere rope by Yashoda.

Go forth with the purity of mind, body, and spirit, offer Him flowers, prostrate, and sing his praises while meditating upon him in heart and mind."

Upon witnessing her hesitation, the poet offers a simple solution.

"Take the name of the Lord, for this action will clear doubts,

flaws, sins, and fear".

With her words, anything magically seems possible. They give the courage to acknowledge flaws within, replace painful patterns with inspiring ones, restore hope one can be the best version of self and celebrate all aspects of this self with the most straightforward mantra. One can aspire higher by infusing divinity in the daily.

"Just as a small cotton piece burns away in a raging inferno with ease, our flaws and misdeeds of the past perish by taking His name."

Andal's verses echo through the corridors of doubt and fears, offering solace, and a roadmap for transcendence. This verse seeks to destroy feelings of disempowerment and replace them with a reclaiming of divine power.

Even a setback is an opportunity to merge into the greatness of the Lord, to immerse in the devotion that flows like a river. Let it cleanse and carry away the debris of self-doubt and fears.

In her words, there's an invitation to surrender, to release the burdens that hold us back. The divine isn't a distant entity but an intimate companion in the journey of self-discovery.

Chapter 11

Segment B

DAY 6

Pullum Silambinakan

The Bird Call

I find myself contemplating why our leader urges the maiden to awaken, observing them engaged in their daily activities.

Yet, as she commences the next verse, a new, conscious rhythm takes hold of me.

"Behold, young maiden, the awakened birds herald the dawn. Can you not hear their joyful chatter? They sing at the temple of our Lord, saluting the king of all birds, Garuda, none other than Lord Vishnu's celestial vehicle. Listen to the resonant call of the sacred, luminous conch blown at the Lord's temple."

Her voice carries a compelling blend of imploration, command, and inspiration.

"Open your eyes, young lass! Krishna's divine play, the Leelas, commenced early. Even as an infant, he triumphed over obstacles like the wicked Putana, who, under Kamsa's orders, offered him

poisoned milk from her teats. He not only extracted the poison but also her life."

She recalls his courageous victory over Sakatasura, the demonic cart that aimed to kill Him. With a single baby toe, He shattered the terrifying demon into pieces.

"Resting serenely on the comforting coils of Adisesha, the snake of infinity, He is the sole cause of the universe. Sages and Yogis, masters of meditation, constantly hold him in their thoughts. They chant the potent name repeatedly, 'Hari, Hari, Hari.' As it reaches a thunderous crescendo, the primordial sound becomes undeniable. Let it penetrate your inner soul. Awaken gently, and let us chant His sacred name together. Allow that sound to refresh our inner selves as we complete the vow."

A brief pause, and then, "Hari, Hari, Hari," echo the sages. We absorb this primordial sound as it swells to a thunderous crescendo. Simply by embracing the two syllables, *Ha*, and Ri, they dispel the darkness of illusion, unleashing the power of this meditative chant. It feels like holding the spirit awareness through meditation.

I am only a drum, but why do my beats reverberate in perfect time? Is there a universal heartbeat? What lies behind the humdrum?

She begins the verse with a few examples of Krishna's childhood feats. Despite immense power, he is easily accessible.

The demons referred to by the poet are allusions to obstacles within us in the form of inactivity, unkind words, unjust acts, gossip, slander, or cruelty. Replacing words with *"Hari"* sparks a quest to higher realms by replacing the painful status quo. The sages, with conches blaring, are reminders to awaken our inner consciousness.

After a few chants, I glance around. The distracted ones are listening keenly. A young girl's eyes sparkle with curiosity. We are piercing through the cacophony of everyday life while resonating with energy.

DAY 7

Keesu Keesengendrum

The Pervasive Twitter

Slender fingers gently beat upon me, awakening me to stir others. Amid the group, there lies a young girl, deeply ensconced in slumber. Despite my earnest efforts, alone, I find it challenging to pierce through the veil of her dreams. Just as I despair, my poet weaves the verse for the day.

"Do you not hear the lively chatter of the valiya birds overhead? They engage in animated conversations, yet you, O girl! You remain in a slumber, seemingly trapped in a trance! The fragrant-haired, flower-bedecked girls vigorously pull at the curd churn, their chunky, coin-like, auspicious jewelry resonating with loud and clear jingles. How can you remain oblivious? The dairymaids, with voices sweet as nectar, sing about Narayana, and Keshava as they work diligently. How can you, a leader among girls, linger in bed? With a countenance that beams with pleasantness, we implore you to open the door."

This verse serves as a gentle awakening for those lingering in a trance, entangled in the material world. Indolence and a sluggish mind and body prevent the girl from rising, and Andal, with her poetic nudges, aims to guide her toward spiritual consciousness. She extends an invitation for the inexperienced to unlock the door of the heart and welcome spiritual awareness.

In the grand tapestry of existence, every creature, from the *valiya* bird to the cheerful dairymaid, plays a unique role. Consider the tiny bee, quietly at work, impacting millions by pollinating every third mouthful of the world's food. Despite its perceived insignificance in size, the bee holds great potential, and its absence would create a massive negative impact on other creatures.

The poet invites us to find joy, cooperation, productivity, and teamwork in our respective roles. She advocates infusing the mundane with an awareness of the divine, transforming the daily grind into a source of bliss and adding an extra layer of significance to the ordinary.

DAY 8

Keezh Vaanam Vellendru

The Bright Eastern Sky

The poet skillfully unveils the heroic tales of the Supreme, crafting verses that dance like gentle whispers to the lingering maidens. The sun is rising and shining, but the girl slumbers.

"O maiden, behold the eastern sky ablaze, as cows, and buffaloes graze in the morning light. Though eager to depart, a few of us detain our companions, yearning to rouse you into the embrace of joy.

Awaken, dear one! Let our voices harmonize in pursuit of the desired blessing. We shall extol him for vanquishing the equine horror, tearing apart the monstrous jaws that once menaced the world. Praise him for subduing wicked wrestlers, dispatched with a deadly pact.

Narayana reigns supreme. Let us bow before him, as he listens to our woes, responding with compassionate 'Ahs and Ahas,' assuring us of his attentive ear. Seek we must, the divine grace of the God of gods, unraveling the mysteries of our spiritual selves."

Epic narratives unfold to reveal supreme grandeur, reminding us that a trace of heroic mettle resides within, as children of the divine. She recounts the tale of the horse-like ogre. Keshi, a monstrous horse wreaking havoc on earth and skies, challenges Krishna to a duel. Krishna emerges victorious by thrusting his arm into Keshi's equine mouth and expanding it infinitely, leading to Keshi's defeat.

The wicked wrestlers referred to are Canura and Mushtika sent by Krishna's evil uncle, Kamsa. Krishna, along with his brother, effortlessly defeats and vanquishes the malevolent duo.

The poet, in a poetic flourish, addresses the maiden's slumber, a metaphor for spiritual unawareness. Amidst verses that sing of Krishna's valor against inner demons, Andal persuades the lingering maiden with tales of the divine warrior.

While both cows and buffaloes share bovine kinship, the poet contrasts their homeward journeys. Buffaloes, with deliberate pauses, wade through pools before returning. Acknowledging diverse personalities, the poet urges maidens to emulate the promptness of cows, reaching the Supreme abode before his awakening. In this, reciprocity, and understanding blossom.

The poet hints at inner awakening, recognizing obstacles within. Even if one strays or tarries, the destination remains steadfast. Slaying external and internal hindrances, we can realign with our true path.

VERSE 9

Thoomani Maadaththu

In Your Well-appointed BowerHere, we stand at the threshold of the reluctant damsel's domain. She remains oblivious to the inner summons within her opulent, aesthetically pleasing world, perhaps eluding the divine due to the esoteric nature of instruction. She is only an unlettered damsel. Is it not the work cut out for devoted scholars?

I am but a messenger, a vibrating medium, yet driven to unravel why my poet urges her to abandon this cocoon of material pleasure.

She takes me up, and I pulsate with her verse.

"O cherished niece, in your lavishly adorned chamber, bedecked with finery, and pearls, your eyes succumb to slumber. The soft glow of beautiful lamps dances around you, and the fragrance of incense drifts toward your inviting bed. We beseech you to unlatch the bejeweled door."

As the girl dismisses the call, the poet queries her mother.

"Dear Aunt, is your daughter struck mute, or has she lost the sense of hearing? Is she lethargic, or ensnared by some colossal spell?"

Unsatisfied with the response, the poet turns again to the girl.

"The Great Magician, Madhava (another name for Vishnu), resides in Vaikunta. Oh, girl! Invoke His numerous names; only He can free you from this worldly trance."

It often seems easier to burrow beneath the blankets and nestle into the warm embrace of the bed than to comprehend the divine. So why does indulgence occasionally masquerade as deprivation? The individual must be receptive to infusing spirituality into everyday work and life. When sleep and ignorance dull the sense organs, what purpose do they serve? Extra baggage weighs down the sparkling soul, hindering the flow of energy. The nature of energy is movement, and this power, now sluggish, is obstructed.

Finding no answer, the poet turns to her aunt for clarity. Is her daughter impaired in hearing or speech? Could she be under a spell, rendering her voiceless? What explains this profound slumber?

Recognizing that the Master Magician possesses infinite facets, the poet introduces another avatar, Madhava.

Who is this Madhava?

Madhava stems from two Sanskrit words, 'Ma' and 'Dhava.' 'Dhava' denotes the consort of, and 'Ma' refers to Goddess Lakshmi, the universal mother provider. As the girls pledge bridal vows, she invokes this name for the One and only. Lakshmi, the goddess of wealth, embodies the spiritual, compassionate, and material wealth enjoyed by Madhava. With Lakshmi in his heart, devotees worshiping Madhava gain easy access to her abundance.

Madhava also signifies the slayer of the demon Madhu. The indulgence the girl displays is the demon hindering her from a rich and complete life. Thus, the poet implores her to annihilate the demon of sloth, indulgence, and laziness, opening her eyes to the natural treasures of existence.

I may be a drum, but I resonate with her verse, drawing parallels. The materials shaping me are diverse and impermanent. Often, those immersed in the luxurious material world resist leaving its comforts. This mindset is a trance. Someday, the very world they perceive as permanent will compel them out. If there is one enduring truth, I will seek it in my innermost vibration.

DAY 10

Notru Chuvargam

Heavenly Vow

Within my little heart, a newfound understanding reverberates as I reach for something beyond the ordinary. Objects once gleaming now appear lackluster, their value fluctuating with time and perspective. Perceptions and objects, like chapters of a story, transition through stages, eventually becoming irrelevant, fading, decaying, or meeting their demise.

Does a sense of a roadmap unfold before me? The once-obscured path begins to reveal itself. Some are fortunate to be aware from birth, while others uncover it along the way. Those familiar with this unseen journey can chart it for others, though, ultimately, it remains a personal choice.

Will the girls choose this path?

"Oh, my dear girl, we embark on this vow to ascend to a higher realm. Why do you remain silent, refusing to open the doors or acknowledge our persistent knocks? Doesn't the fragrance of the tulasi herb garland evoke memories of His fragrant hair? We praise His courage and virtue, the one who bestows upon us the divine drum. Remember the day when He triumphed over the demon Kumbakarna? Has this demon cast upon you the grand sleep before meeting his demise? Oh, damsel! Recognize your jewel-like essence among us. Awaken from your slumber, open the doors, and realize the One."

In this verse, the maiden seems unwilling and overshadowed by others in various stages of awakening, and her slumber takes precedence. The poet draws a parallel with the ogre Kumbhakarna from the Ramayana, cursed to a six-month-long deep sleep annually. Narratives, metaphors, and legends serve the purpose of engaging the mind, yet the call to embrace higher consciousness must be voluntary.

Enveloped in the indulgences of the transient world, the girl clings to her familiar reality, seemingly oblivious to the impermanence that shrouds it. The poet skillfully nudges readers to ponder the adequacy of material comforts in addressing profound inner needs. What unfolds when the once-abundant material wealth transforms into constraining attachments, fostering discontent despite excessive indulgence?

The poet gently references the concept of heaven, transcending its traditional afterlife notion. Within the earthly journey, the girls are guided by the poet's roadmap, urging an elevation of present life above considerations of the afterlife. While reveling in the joys of material comforts, the poet provocatively questions their capacity to satiate the yearning for something profoundly enchanting.

Referring to the slumbering damsel as a jewel, the poet sees a sparkling potential within, hoping she awakens to claim it. The fragrance in the sacred basil leaf adorning His hair symbolizes the creative spirit, aligning with Krishna's knowledge of the Absolute in Chapter 7.9 of the Bhagavad Gita. The poet portrays divine allure, creativity, generosity, and magnificence, emphasizing that incorporating spirituality enriches present life with sweetness and bliss.

There is a reason for narratives, metaphors, and legends—they engage the mind. However, the call to engage in higher consciousness must come voluntarily. The poet alludes to heaven not just for an afterlife; the girls are within the earthly life journey, and she provides a roadmap for elevating the present over the after. The poet acknowledges that material comforts delight the senses but questions whether these alone are sufficient to connect to something more significant. A dehydrated person in a desert can write off a kingdom and riches for one drop of water, and life's tests demonstrate the fickle worth of material wealth.

Describing the slumbering damsel as a jewel, the poet poignantly recognizes a radiant potential within, yearning for her awakening to embrace and dance with it. In this verse, the sparkling jewel represents the same precious essence that comprises the Supreme. The metaphor echoes the profound connection between the individual soul and the divine, encouraging the recognition of the inherent divinity within every being. It signifies not only the individual's unique essence but also the universal truth that binds all existence. Incorporating the spiritual into daily life elevates the present moment to a state of sweet richness, where every aspect of the self is celebrated in heavenly contentment.

DAY 11

Katru Karavai

Milch Cows

Sensuality intertwines with the human experience—a thread woven into the fabric of our existence. In this pasuram, Andal gently nudges the deeply slumbering maiden to recognize beauty beyond the fleeting.

"O slender lass, akin to a golden creeper, your Venusian mount holds the allure of sensuality, reminiscent of a cobra's hood. Yet, adorned with the beauty of a forest peacock, why persist in this somnolence?"

The allusion to sleep isn't in the closing of her eyes but in her languid repose upon the comfortable bed.

"You hail from a lineage of mistresses tending to fertile herds. The Mighty One effortlessly subdues foes without marching to war. We know him as the simple Govinda, the flawless king of cowherds. You, fortunate to share his lineage.

Rise and join your kin and friends; we gather in your inner courtyard. Let us sing and invoke the name of the One resembling a dark rain cloud, our Mugilvannan.

O possessor of wealth, why persist in a trance so deep, where you neither speak nor stir?"

In the contemplation of the poet's intention, fundamental questions arise, probing the nature of permanence in the realm of sensual pleasures. Does the allure of physical beauty endure, or does it succumb to the relentless march of time? Can immortal forms of beauty and sweetness transcend the ephemeral nature of fleeting pleasures, and do these enduring gifts shape the core of one's identity?

The narrative unfolds with the tangible portrayal of a slumbering maiden, adorned with physical allure, charm, power, and wealth. However, the poet subtly alludes to the act of sleep as a trance, hinting at a deeper, more profound state of being. While the verse acknowledges the inherent blessings of savoring sensory pleasures and material prosperity, it also underscores their temporal and inconsistent nature. Physical beauty inevitably fades, material wealth fluctuates, and the transient nature of sensual pleasures evolves over time. Rather than merely counting these external blessings, the poet encourages the maiden to imbue her existence with the depth of the highest spirit, an enduring source of meaning and purpose.

The verse serves as a wake-up call, urging a conscious awareness of the impermanence inherent in concrete abundance. The rhythmic drumbeats resonate with the intent to awaken those in slumber, delivering a message that transcends the fleeting nature of external gratifications. Sensual pleasures are integral to existence, and the poet hints at true intimacy with a fusion of sensuality and divinity.

Existence, as the poet articulates, unfolds in three modes—tamasic immersion in material riches and the tumult of *rajasic* energies, offering the choice to delve deeper into a spiritual realm or embrace the *sattvic* reality. The sleeping maiden, in her current state, is influenced by the mode of *"tamas"* (inertia), which is characterized by a lack of spiritual awareness. The hint of *"rajas"* implies that the maiden might also be driven by desires, passions, and a sense of restlessness, contributing to her state of slumber. The poet encourages the maiden to move towards the mode of *"sattva,"* which represents balance, purity, and spiritual illumination while enjoying sensual and material abundance.

The metaphor of the cowherd guides the damsel toward a transformative choice. In the mode of ignorance, one may remain oblivious to the boundless grass at their feet. Alternatively, the poet advocates for infusing spiritual sweetness into daily life, akin to a cow grazing freely with contentment. This choice fosters strength, acceptance, and connection preparing one to navigate life's gifts and disappointments with grace. There is a feeling of being supported by the universe. The realization dawns that **Govinda**, the Ultimate Cowherd, encapsulates the profound truth underlying this transformative journey.

VERSE 12

Kanaithilam Katrerumai

Compassionate Bovine Mother

Here, in numbers, we gather at the gates of another prosperous maiden, surrounded by material abundance. Yet, there is a spiritual ignorance and a type of resistance in her. Andal addresses this reluctance with her woven verse for the day.

"The mother buffalo, sensing her hungry calf, releases copious milk from swollen udders without resistance. Prosperous sister! In your possession is such a willing creature, transforming the courtyard into sludgy earth with her abundant outpouring. As the early morning fog drips, we stand in the cold, clinging to the threshold of your courtyard door. We sing of Him who valiantly vanquished the enemy king from Lanka. Why will you not try opening your lips in His praise to experience the sweetness in your heart? We implore you to arise from slumber and savor this sweetness. So why do you resist so?"

The poet skillfully contrasts the willing and the resistant. The willing, despite the cold, hang on the wooden ledges in a sludgy courtyard, their hearts open to savor the divine love pouring forth.

Praising the Lord for intolerance toward inimical qualities, the poet illustrates the consequence in Ravana. Once an ardent devotee blessed with immense power, his misuse led to divine intervention.

Rich analogies in the poem unfold with layers of meaning. First, the mother cow involuntarily releases milk while looking hither and thither to feed her hungry calves. Second, the abundant milk turns the grounds into sodden earth. The poet encourages listeners to expand this analogy to view this from their worldly prism. Third, the running milk is abundant material wealth upon viewing the mother as a "cash cow." Fourth, the willingness to release milk without a pull is akin to openness to letting in spiritual abundance. Finally, the maternal love the animal feels towards her missing children is comparable to the love the Divine has for the creations.

Girls cling to wooden support, avoiding sinking too deep into the glut of material sludge. Their goal is clear, as they opt to open their minds to divine influx. The cold fog presents an obstacle to their vow.

At the concrete level, such discomfort invites staying within bed covers. Yet, the young devotees view this as an exercise to dispel the fog of ignorance and reveal awareness. The blanket is reluctance, illusion, and ignorance covering the permanence.

Viewing him as the ultimate cowherd of souls, devotees trust him like baby calves, yet they are willing as the generous mother buffalo, releasing milk at the mere thought of her calf.

Nonplussed, I too wonder. With strength in numbers, the motivated gather at the gates of another prosperous young maiden. She possesses material abundance. Yet, why is she spiritually resistant?

DAY 13

Pullinvai Keendanai

The One who Destroyed the Beaked Demon

As her fingers quicken, I resonate at a marching pace, echoing Andal's desire to awaken a damsel who rationalizes her slumber. The maiden believes that dreaming of Him from the comfort of her bed alone suffices. Even as a humble drum, I acknowledge the challenge of attaining the Courageous One. The Lord's gift to the cosmos is infinite, demanding reciprocal effort from devotees.

Andal embarks on a new verse, praising Him, and drawing from two great epics, the Ramayana and Mahabharata, in her attempt to awaken her friend.

"We gather here, singing praises of the Valiant One who defeated the demon assuming a massive heron-like form. With ease, the brave spirit ripped open the terrorizing monster's beak, much like his conquest of the evil Ravana and similar ogres. Venus has arisen this early morning, and Jupiter has vanished from the sky.

O beautiful girl, with doe-like eyes rimmed red like bees atop a flower! Do you not hear the twittering birds? Why ignore our heartfelt call to dip in the cool, cleansing water? Why pretend to sleep in your fragrant bed? Cease playing this tricky game, attempting to hold on to Krishna for you alone. Join us in fulfilling this vow."

The poet's verses intricately weave a tapestry of spiritual and moral lessons, drawing profound inspiration from the timeless epics Ramayana and Mahabharata. Through the symbolic representations of Jatayu and Bakasura, the poet delves into the duality of kindness and cruelty, prompting introspection on the internal struggle to channel positive attributes while shedding negativity. This exploration resonates with the poet's emphasis on combating both external evils and internal obstacles through the virtues of divinity and courage, mirroring the valiant efforts of Jatayu in confronting injustice.

The interpretation of war extends beyond the physical battlefield, encapsulating the internal struggles against personal demons and negativity. Drawing parallels with the epics, the verses serve as metaphors for the heroic journey of confronting and defeating inner obstacles. The call to not cower in the face of injustice resonates with the ethos of facing life's challenges with unwavering bravery and determination. The deliberate effort and commitment required to eliminate impediments, whether superficial roadblocks or profound personal challenges, align with the multifaceted nature of the ongoing struggle.

On a practical, everyday level, the verses underscore the pivotal role of choice in various facets of life, including goal completion, time management, hygiene, the importance of dialog over duel, and overall well-being. The symbolism of the girl's reluctance to leave her warm covers reflects a broader theme of resistance to change, attachment to old habits, or a lack of awareness of the inherent transformative power.

The poet's encouragement to replace negativity with praise for the divine power and to take a cleansing dip signifies a resolute commitment to spiritual growth and the initiation of a transformative journey. The concept of destroying personal demons and addressing past mistakes aligns seamlessly with the overarching theme of awakening the hero within—an individual capable of overcoming challenges through noble thoughts and positive actions.

In the simplest way, the poet conveys the concept of just and unjust wars. She expounds with simplicity the words Krishna conveyed to Arjuna in the Bhagavad Gita starting with restraint. The evolution of *ahimsa* or non-violence from its roots in ancient dharmic religions to a contemporary humanitarian ideal underscores its enduring relevance in advocating for peace amidst the seemingly violent complexities of the world. Together, these perspectives inspire profound introspection on choice, worthiness, and the transformative power inherent within everyone's spiritual and ethical journey.

The Bhagavad Gita, a sacred Hindu scripture, presents a nuanced perspective on the necessity of war, emphasizing the concept of dharma (righteous duty) and the ethical considerations surrounding armed conflict. In the Gita, Lord Krishna imparts profound teachings to the warrior Arjuna on the battlefield of Kurukshetra, where he grapples with the moral dilemma of participating in a war against his own relatives. Krishna urges Arjuna to fulfill his duty as a warrior without attachment to the fruits of his actions. The teachings underscore the importance of fighting for justice, righteousness, and the protection of dharma. The valiant Jatayu tried to preserve dharma by protecting Sita against Ravana.

In this context, the necessity of war is not glorified for its own sake, but rather to uphold moral order and righteousness.

The poet realizes there are other paths to spiritual realization, including the path of knowledge, devotion, and selfless action. While engaging in war is presented as a specific duty for a warrior, the overarching message of the Gita is to transcend the dualities of pleasure and pain, success and failure, and to attain a state of equanimity and spiritual realization. With this simple verse, the poet delves into a complex concept like war that plagues us even today.

DAY 14

Ungal Puzhakadai

Your Backyard

A profound transformation is underway – a shift from resistance to openness, from hesitation to receptivity. The once hesitant and unaware are now fully prepared to receive. The girls, who were once passive, are now holding one of their own accountable for not living up to the commitment of awakening the sleeping.

"In the pond of your backyard, the red flowers are in full bloom. However, those night-blooming water lilies have closed their petals firmly. Can you even see this?

With white teeth, the sages in their brick-colored clothing depart to the temple to blow their conches. You are the illumined motivator, waking us up with praises for the divine. You're the incomparable Nangai, the One with good qualities. Where is your guilt for having such a tongue? First, you tell us to awaken, and then you slumber. Now it is our responsibility to remind the leader to awaken. Continue to sing the praises of the Lotus-eyed One who holds the white conch and the brilliant discus with ease in either hand."

This verse serves as a reminder to the girls about the importance of keeping their word. The mention of the sages with sparkling teeth indicates their clean habits where healthy bodies, minds, and spirits thrive. To be a leader, one must inspire.

On a deeper note, the leader faces the group's question. Is she caught up in the noble act of waking up others? Has she slowed down, or did she let go of the undivided focus on the divine? Is she upholding her word or relinquishing it in slumber?

The leader, with infectious zeal, rallied the group. No longer a mere drum, I resonate with the devotion she instills in everyone and everything. She has kindled spirituality within her friends, and the spark has grown into a flame. The tides have turned, and now they question the leader's level of commitment.

The poet's imagery of flowers and the sun vividly illustrates the Supreme One, akin to the sun, witnessing the blossoming lotuses under merciful rays. The girls, now resembling fully bloomed red lotuses, both receive and reflect the beauty and warmth of this benevolence. The students, thoroughly enthused, implore their leader to fully open her mind and not withdraw like night lilies to the sun, urging her to surrender to spiritual magnanimity. This verse captures their new mindset of engagement, urgency, and accountability in the quest for the divine.

As the dawn breaks, the devotees, like wide-open red flowers, are ready to receive. Now fully awakened, they gently rebuke their leader, emphasizing the concept of accountability with the plea, "Practice what you preach, sister!"

True teachers value students who remind them of the quest's purpose, and accountable involvement enhances mutual trust. In this intimate moment, as she holds me close, her heartbeats resonate with the repetition of the sacred name, revealing her inner satisfaction. Despite being near, she gracefully allows her followers to gently rebuke her, recognizing their newfound urgency to connect with the Supreme. In a subtle yet profound shift, the followers unintentionally assume leadership, and she quietly supports them in leading.

DAY 15

Elle Ilankiliye

Hark, Young Parrot!

Within each of us resides that one girl, convinced that no one can sing the highest praise better than her. She prefers to engage in solitary devotion, confident in her knowledge of scriptures, Vedas, and mantras. This maiden believes herself to be more awakened than others, setting the stage for a dialog orchestrated by Andal between her and the entreating group.

Group: "Young lady, as beautiful as a colorful parrot, are you still languishing in bed?"

Girl: "Oh girls, you are shrill in speech. I will come, but it will be on my own time."

Group: "Commendable are those clever words, but you are transparently prevaricating."

Girl: "Well, you have admirable traits, and I need to be left alone."

Group: "Why must it be different for you? Make haste and join us."

Girl: "Has everyone then set out?"

Group: "Yes, everyone has departed, and is assembling for the vow. Come outside, grace us with your presence, and honor us by taking a head count. Awaken, and let us sing of Him. Let us sing about the single-minded One who conquered the gigantic, hostile elephant Kuvalayapida. Together, we will sing his praise. He is the One who can remove the enmity from enemies. Therefore, let us sing together in recognition of this exalted enchanter."

This verse delves into the theme of conviction, questioning the strength of devotion. Using the mutual dialog theme, the poet constructs this poem.

Do you, at times, recognize that girl within yourself? This young lass is hesitant to embrace the group's intent fully. She speaks with a hint of sarcasm, believing her devotion is best expressed by singing alone about the resting Lord. Why does she resist joining the group? Is something vital missing? Does she feel that solitary worship is superior?

At every step, the collective group has embraced selflessness as the ultimate check. Energies merge when the individual devotee sheds his/her ego to contribute to the greater good.

"Why must it be different for you?" This question becomes a key to understanding individual ego.

The reference to Krishna as the slayer of the hostile elephant Kuvalayapida adds depth to the discourse. Krishna faced the enraged elephant sent by Kamsa to kill him. The already raging elephant was goaded further by the mahout to turn all his senses to the senseless act of hostility. Removing personal ego is akin to disarming the internal rage, turning it into devotion, and love. Despite internal virtues, ego can cause great harm.

The poet also touches upon the significance of speech, symbolizing mental discipline, and intellectual caliber. When the girl is called out, she blames the others for shrill speech. Here, the poet reflects on the power of words. Speech should be benevolent, constructive, and ego-free. When there is a call to action, there is no need for excuses or projection. One must act.

The group presents a united front, heralding the divine as an enchanting magician capable of removing negative qualities, even in enemies. This highlights the importance of shedding hatred and surrendering to the master magician.

The debate convinces not only the individual girl but the entire group about the importance of shedding ego, sweetness in speech, promoting kindness, and recognizing strength in unity. The verse emphasizes clearing the "mine and thine" attitude, for the goal is to surrender to the sublime. It implies that when the Lord shares love with devotees, divinity is amplified. Love is not a possession, but a force nurtured, cultivated, and shared freely.

Peeling away the final layers of resistance, the poet underscores the importance of unity in absorbing and incorporating divinity. The girls, united in kinship, can no longer delay their collective journey.

Chapter 12

Segment C

VERSE 16

Nayakanai Nindra

The Standing Gatekeeper

The spiritually ignited girls stand at the threshold of the palace, a symbolic juncture in their quest. Their journey, marked by deep introspection, has equipped them with an energetic enthusiasm that emanates from profound inquiry. Contemplating the material and immaterial, permanence, and impermanence, illusion, and reality, they have dismantled internal stumbling blocks, preparing to fully engage with the divine.

However, the portal presents a new challenge – is the Supreme Being ready to receive them?

Having refreshed themselves in the chilly waters, the girls, and I arrive at the holy temple where *Emperuman* or the mighty Lord rests with his family. As their heartbeat synchronizes with mine, a pulsating chorus echoes, "We fixate upon the Lord."

Our initial encounter is with the temple guard, a beautifully adorned yet formidable obstacle. The physical proximity heightens the girls' anticipation, and I resonate with the rhythmic expectancy in their hearts. Eager to break barriers and receive grace, they approach the guard with reverence.

The poet, in her wisdom, educates them on the etiquette of entering the sacred premises. Demonstrating empathy, she underscores the importance of respect, advising against barging in unannounced. The girls, understanding this, courteously request entry, explaining their arduous quest, and pledging to follow the required protocol.

Despite the numerical advantage, the girls opt for respect, kindness, and empathy rather than force. Recognizing the guard as a fellow devotee, they patiently convey their journey, and, in a surprising turn, the guard relents. Gratitude fills the hearts of the maidens as they step into the sacred space.

The urgency to reach the Lord is palpable, yet they refrain from thoughtless haste. Instead, they decide to awaken him through divine praises, petitions, and love. The verse introduces Nayaka, the guard, imploring him to lower his defenses and allow entry.

"O Nayaka of Nanda Gopa's palace, guardian of the door adorned with flags and festoons, kindly unlatch the decorated door with bells. We, the innocent devotees from cowherd homes, seek entry. Mannivanan, the Enchanter, promised us protection. After purifying mind, body, and spirit, we wish to gently wake Him from slumber. Please do not turn us away; instead, unlock the doors for us."

Their words, filled with kindness, and sincerity, lead to kind actions. The guard, disarmed by their devotion, unlocks the doors, granting them access.

As we step across the threshold, my heart resonates with anticipation, eager to draw closer to the divine. The poet, once again, alludes to slumber, emphasizing the Lord's unawareness. The girls, newly awakened, prepare to face the challenge of rousing the Enchanter, embodying the belief that faith can move mountains. They stand ready for the test that lies ahead.

VERSE 17

Ambarame Thaneere

Clothes and Water

Finally, we've made it! Breathless, I take in the splendor of the beautiful courtyard as we enter the stately home. Getting to this point was no cakewalk, but the true challenge begins now.

Inside, family members rest in slumber. Nandagopa, the Lord's father, sleeps soundly in the first room, and Yashoda, the mother, in the second. Krishna and Balarama reside in the innermost room. We opt for a room-by-room approach, waking the relatives first, and then the Lord with sincere entreaties.

But how do you reach the divine? There's no roadmap. Somehow, the girls have reached this far. What are the next steps? The girls assess their virtues – kindness, compassion, love, and adherence to dharma. Are these qualities enough, and most importantly, *are **they** enough*?

The appeal begins with the elder. *"O Nandagopa, father of my Lord, philanthropic doer of good deeds, wake up! You generously donate clothing, water, and food to others."*

The poet seizes the opportunity to highlight philanthropy, cultivating habits as a beacon to others, and upholding family unity. The contrast between material and spiritual sustenance is emphasized with gratitude expressed for their sustenance.

The next stanza addresses the mother, Yashoda, a role model for the young lasses.

"Oh, Yashoda, you're the illumined lamp, a beacon for all slender women from the cowherd family. Please wake up."

Mother Yashoda symbolizes wisdom, and her influence is deemed crucial.

The following stanza addresses the Lord's sibling Balarama.

"O blessed brother Baladeva, you sleep with the golden anklet manifesting your prosperity. O Krishna, as Vishnu, the mighty king of Lords, you assumed an extraordinary form and tore up the sky to measure the earth. O Balarama, we implore you to arise with your younger brother Krishna."

Diplomatically attempting to rouse them without rushing in or disregarding occupants, the devotees appeal to the father's charity and the mother's role as a beacon.

The use of the metanarrative sparks contemplation. King Mahabali becomes a symbol of material prosperity, his wealth manifests in gold, currency, and land. Despite his benevolence, his *Asura*, or monster lineage poses a threat to the order of the *devas* or Gods, particularly Indra, the battler of monsters. The Devas, anticipating potential chaos with the ascent of lawless Asuras after Mahabali's virtuous rule, decide to intervene.

Indra's mother leverages her devotion to invoke Vishnu, the preserver. In Vishnu's discernment, Mahabali proves to be a virtuous ruler, his lineage notwithstanding. Rather than conquest, Vishnu chooses a different path—to divest Mahabali of material strength and power, ensuring balance, and preventing demonic dominance. The aim is a profound transformation, a shift toward spiritual liberation.

Vishnu manifests as a young, non-threatening boy as Mahabali celebrates with penances. The generous king, drawn to the lad's charm, offers gifts. The lad requests three pieces of land the size of his foot. Mahabali, true to his word, obliges. Yet, the lad's subsequent expansion into colossal proportions during each step—the first covering the earth, the second reaching heaven—reveals a divine design.

For the third step, Mahabali, having exhausted his land, humbly offers his head. Vishnu places his foot on Mahabali's head, pushing him to the netherworld. This narrative intricately explores the destruction of the ego. Mahabali, willingly surrendering his ego for humility, undergoes instant liberation, attaining Nirvana.

Stories serve as more than tales; they are concrete steps to the abstract spirit. Mahabali, representing material abundance, contrasts with Vishnu's vast form, illustrating the dichotomy between illusion and reality, impermanence, and change. Each step symbolizes distinct states of existence and consciousness, culminating in the last step signifying Moksha—a spiritual liberation from all worlds. As I beat to their plaintive entreaties, I hope the spirit receives our shared message, understanding the profound journey from material wealth to spiritual liberation.

VERSE 18

Undu Madagalitran

Of the One who Subdued Wild Elephants

"O daughter-in-law of the valiant Nandagopala, who subdued elephants in their rut, we beseech you to awaken. Roosters proclaim the dawn with exuberance, and cuckoos serenade on the jasmine trellises, their melodies urging us into wakefulness.

Oh, lady! Your tresses, redolent with the fragrance of sandalwood, grace you with an aura of allure. Kindly extend your benevolence and unlatch the door. Your hands, akin to a delicate pink lotus, possess the power to gently guide the Supreme Lord as if He were a cherished plaything. Yearning to join in the joyous chorus of praises to your Beloved, we implore you to let the stacked bracelets resonate melodiously as you unlatch the door with those petal-soft hands, inviting us within."

In their entreaty to the consort of the Lord, the maidens harbor the hope of a more accessible passage. While the Lord may stand imposing as Narasimha, the man-lion avatar that vanquished the malevolent Hiranyakashapu with unparalleled strength and cunning, Nappinai, his mistress, wields an even greater influence. At times, he assumes a role akin to an acquiescent ball within her seemingly lotus-like hands.

The poet directly engages with the beloved consort, urging her to employ her delicate, feminine, yet influential hands. The devotees yearn for the resounding jingle of multiple bracelets as the Lord's mistress graciously opens the sacred door, ushering them into the divine presence.

Within the feminine essence of divinity lies *daya*, or compassion. Hence, the spirit of the Lord seeks equilibrium by merging with the compassionate heart of the consort.

The Lord and His consort are indivisible, prompting the maidens to appeal to her for access. This symbolic plea underscores the pivotal role of compassion in elevating devotion to consciousness.

In various realms, this verse continues to wield profound influence, echoing its significance in myriad ways.

Centuries later, the venerable Ramanuja echoed this verse during his contemplative walks, entreating Napinnai to unfold the spiritual realm. His profound devotion to Andal led him to frequently recite her verses, a practice that significantly shaped his reverence for the Goddess Mahalakshmi and extended to his interactions with other women.

Approaching the door of his guru, Periya Nambi, Ramanuja intoned the closing lines of the verse, "With bracelets jingling on your lotus-like hands, please arise to open the door." Miraculously, the door swung open, revealing the guru's daughter, Athuzha, standing at the threshold. Witnessing this divine encounter, the great seer Ramanuja, overwhelmed by reverence, prostrated himself at the feet of the young maiden.

Puzzled by Ramanuja's act, the guru inquired why he bowed before a youthful maiden. Ramanuja attributed his gesture to the profound impact of Andal's verses. The maiden's presence reminded him of the divine consort, prompting his humble surrender. Recognizing the potency of the poet's words, the guru astutely referenced the verse, asking, *"Undu*

Mathagalithan anusanthanamo?"—Is this the effect of the sacred verse?

The poet's words weave enchantment through their simplicity, advocating the dharmic path as a straightforward guide to infuse spirituality into life. The once formidable obstacle course transforms into a leveled path, offering a direct route to divinity for those immersed in its deeper nuances.

VERSE 19

Kuttu Vilakeriya

As the Tall Lamp Burns

A gentle radiance envelops the bower, where the Lord, and His consort repose in tranquil intimacy, the softly burning lamp casting a romantic glow.

In stark contrast, outside in the cold, misty morning, the girls await a glimpse of the Lord. Their first appeal is to Nappinai, the consort, recognizing that to reach the Lord's empathetic gaze, they must first engage with her. They draw attention to the sharp contrast between their harsh surroundings and her cozy abode, where the Lord is entwined in her infinite charms.

Gradually, the realization dawns on me. The Lord and His consort share an intimate space, nestled in a comfortable boudoir, wrapped in the warmth of their divine connection.

The girls beseech Nappinai for the Lord's omnipresence, echoing the verses of the poet. My beating heart resonates with the fervency of their pleas.

"The gently burning oil lamp illuminates your surroundings, where you repose on an opulent bed with ivory posts. The cotton mattress beneath you offers unparalleled softness."

Oh, Nappinai, adorned with clusters of fragrant flowers in your lovely hair. Unperturbed by our appeals, you remain immersed in love".

In this way, the poet calls upon the fragrant consort to facilitate their access before shifting entreaties to the universe's Lover.

"Oh, broad-shouldered Lord! Your eyes find comfort upon her generous bosom. Why the silent repose? Speak to us."

A trace of accusation colors their words as they turn back to Nappinai.

"Oh, beautiful Nappinai, eyes adorned with collyrium, how long will you captivate him? He is ensnared by your charms, oblivious to our presence. Can you not release him, even for a fleeting moment?

Can't you see the injustice? Is this befitting of you? We cannot accept this."

Faced with Nappinai's unresponsiveness, the girls attempt to convey the injustice of withholding the Lord in exclusivity. They recognize the enchantment she holds over Him and lament the unfairness of monopolizing attention.

The vivid imagery unfolds, allowing us to witness the divine couple on the luxurious *Panchashayanam* bed. In the corner, a lamp with five wicks burns gently, casting an intimate warmth over the sacred scene.

The potency of her words is akin to observing the ethereal scene of intimacy. The bed, adorned with mattresses filled with swan and peacock feathers, fragrant herbs, the softest cotton, and scented petals, stands elevated in divine opulence. A lamp with five wicks delicately burns in the corner, casting a tender, and intimate glow that permeates the sacred space.

This symbolic portrayal of the bridal union serves as a tangible representation of an abstract spiritual fusion. As an illustrative example, a newlywed bride often receives a Kuthu vilakku, an oil lamp with five wicks swimming in oil, symbolizing her marital responsibilities.

Upon entering a new home, the first wick serves as a reminder of the duty to nurture, preserve, and sustain love within the family. The devotees, standing in the cold fog, juxtapose their discomfort with her warm cocoon of love shared with the Lord. Emphasizing their non-possessive nature, they express a desire to partake in divine love.

The second wick symbolizes patience towards the new family members with their unique faces and ways. The girls appeal to her to manifest this patience by not making them wait for the Lord's attention.

The third wick signifies intelligence and wisdom. The devotees implore her to recognize that the Lord's love transcends beyond their immediate circle, encompassing the entire universe. Their souls, too, yearn for profound spiritual union.

The fourth wick represents the bride's resoluteness in fulfilling familial responsibilities. The young ladies, standing firm in their quest, question if the Lord's consort mirrors the same commitment.

The fifth wick reminds the bride to choose appropriate actions in various situations. As she engages in her duties, they inquire if she upholds the values of love, patience, intelligence, and resoluteness in the face of discomfort. The Lord may be under her spell, yet she is urged not to confine His grace solely to herself. Their plea underscores the need for accountability towards devotees enduring discomfort while awaiting His divine grace, which is intended for all creations.

VERSE 20

Muppathu Muvvar

Thirty Million (A Large Following)

Appeals and Entreaties

In this poignant verse, the devotees direct their appeals to two central figures: Krishna and his consort Nappinai, imploring them to shower a divine cascade of merciful love upon the supplicants.

Approaching Krishna with the simplicity befitting cowherd women, the devotees delicately awaken the sacred spirit, desiring a loving union without disrupting his divine routine. Their plea is devoid of material aspirations—fame, fortune, power, or beauty. Instead, they seek to emulate his ultimate consort in a spiritual union, transcending the mundane.

The verse unfolds with praises for Krishna preceding those for Napinnai, the divine consort. The devotees, adopting the roles of devoted wives, request a fan, and a mirror—objects symbolic of the service in a marital ritual. Showering sincere praises upon Napinnai, they acknowledge her as the quintessential woman who can awaken Krishna's awareness to the multitude of devotees.

Addressing Krishna, they sing,

"O Valiant Sri Krishna, leader, savior, and protector of three hundred thirty million demigods or devas, please awaken from your slumber. You are omnipresent, preemptively shielding the devas from harm. Your impartial and immense strength safeguards

devotees, inflicting sorrow on enemies. Arise to extend your protective grace to us."

Turning to Napinnai, they depict her *"with tender breasts resembling golden cones and coral lips, embodying the epitome of femininity, Lakshmi (Periya Piratti)."*

The devotees beseech her, *"Please awaken! Gently rouse your husband with the fan and present him with the mirror. Permit him to bathe us in the shower of his mercy."*

As their devotion deepens, the devotees earn Nappinai's favor. She, moved by their tenacity, love, and unadulterated devotion, acknowledges the purity in their plea. Her approval signifies the solidification of their case to attain the Supreme. The girls' passionate pursuit has purged undesirable traits, paving the way for Nappinai to intervene on their behalf. Recognizing their unselfish devotion, she begins to advocate for their cause.

The concept of offering to the Divine suggests a profound understanding that all the gifts and blessings we possess ultimately belong to the source. It emphasizes the idea that there is no need to cling tightly to these gifts, as they are granted by the benevolence of the giver. By offering back to the divine, one expresses gratitude for the abundance received. This practice encourages a sense of detachment and a recognition of the divine as the ultimate source of all that we have.

Within the temple rituals, realia serve as offerings to the Lord, symbolizing devotion. Devotees give form to the Formless, creating an outer sacred space to connect to the inner sacred space. Lamps illuminate dispelling ignorance, incense elevates the sense of smell, clothing, and jewelry adorn, flowers, and sandal paste cool, while grains, and aromatic oils are presented to quell the hunger of the soul. The symbolic fan and mirror, sought by the devotees, signify a desire to serve the Lord akin to his consort. They pledge to extend this service beyond personal benefit, intending to share the cooling breeze as a service to the world.

The mirror, reflecting without absorption, becomes a metaphor for navigating the transient joys and sorrows of earthly life with awareness. The mirror shows everything, so there's full knowledge of the temporary. Emotions, viewed as mere reflections, neither absorb beauty, nor flaw—an insightful perspective on the impermanence of worldly experiences.

Chapter 13

Segment D

DAY 21

Etra Kalangal Edhir Pongi

The Brimming Milkpails

Faced with the fervent outpouring of love from the devoted assembly, Nappinai finds herself unable to resist. How could she withhold the pure devotion emanating from them? There is but one course she joyfully embraces—the role of an ardent devotee herself. Willingly relinquishing her position as consort, she ascends to the *higher* status of a sincere worshiper.

Confronted with this collective and unalloyed love, Nappinai transcends possessive thoughts of exclusively having the Lord. The pure devotion radiating from the group is unparalleled. Becoming a part of this energetic flow, she recognizes that sole possessiveness can never match the heights of boundless love that emanate collectively. With her inclusion, the Lord is bound to awaken.

Nappinai symbolizes Lakshmi, the goddess of wealth, and compassion. Stripping away the goddess aspect leaves people pondering the fickleness of wealth or the absence of compassion in times of need. The true reason Lakshmi is a goddess of abundance is because she thrives in permanence, choosing to stay only with devotees who wholeheartedly and unselfishly love the Supreme.

In this realm, the supreme power is referred to as Narayana. Despite the plethora of esoteric Vedas and Upanishads aimed at understanding this reality or the nature of pure consciousness, divinity remains easily understood. Supreme bliss and inner consciousness emerge when the mind, body, and spirit align with sattvic and dharmic principles. The realization comes through practice, highlighting that benevolence surrounds us. In this context, Narayana's avatar is Krishna, whose love, and kindness flow ceaselessly, akin to the unending milk from the engorged udders of benevolent cows.

His benevolence extends to all, not confined to a select group of devotees. Even the most heinous enemies, upon choosing the divine path, experience transformative amity through his merciful kindness. Corrosive hate is absolved through complete surrender, transmuting into the purest love.

"Abundant milk flows incessantly from the generous udders of the solid and healthy cows. The pails cannot contain such abundance, so the milk runs all over.

O Son of the accomplished Nandagopa! Please awaken! The supreme texts of Vedas describe you as Omnipotent. Please make your glory visible to us, simple cowherds, in a fashion we can also understand. Oh, Supreme Lord! You show yourself to your devotees in various ways. Oh, glowing beacon! We implore you to wake up for us.

Even your enemies surrender at your feet with realization. That action alone is a victory from the pain of enmity. You are their final refuge when they come helpless at your feet. Indeed, can you not conquer over simple lasses like us? We come to your doorstep with nothing but devotion. We aim to laud your glory and surrender in love to you completely."

This *Pasuram* vividly portrays the unadulterated devotion of the *Gopikas* or devoted cowherd lasses. Though the Vedas may seem esoteric, their truth is inherently simple: to become divine is to love wholly and completely. The poet underscores that even in their innocent cowherd world, the unlettered young lasses understand the essence. Their actions mirror relentless devotion, seeking surrender, and conquest by the love of the Lord. In the presence of the Lord, material wealth, wars, glory, and fame, as they have known them, attain a different meaning. The journey must continue until they shed the scintilla of ego.

DAY 22

Anganmanyalathil Arasar

The Monarchs of this Big Beautiful World

Andal commenced the journey as a leader and teacher, but her strength truly shines brighter as a devotee within this assembly, weaving poetic imagery to unravel the incomprehensible. The Lord, gratified by her transformative eulogy, bestows upon them divine regard.

Her eloquent expressions spotlight the potency of devotees and their yearning for the benevolent gaze of acknowledgment. Abandoning egos, bonds, and possessions, the devotees plead for unity. Like disarmed royal kings, they submit themselves before the feet of a mighty emperor.

Surrender, paradoxically, embodies independent will. It may sound peculiar, akin to great kings conceding battles to secure a victory in the war. Yet, here I am, contributing my beats to an unknown majesty. I do not feel insignificant, for I am part of something magnificent. We gather with our voices, faculties, and gratitude to extol this grace giver. The poet initiates the verse with this metaphor.

"Like proud kings humbled in this beautiful world, we too surrender completely at the foot of your reclining throne. Ego obliterated, we approach in a line, heads bowed, seeking your refuge."

The poet then entreats the Lord as a devotee to gradually unveil divine eyes. Recognizing that the devotees may struggle with the full intensity of grace all at once, the plea is for a slow initiation of the gaze.

"Will you not open your red, intense eyes ever so slowly to let us into your line of vision? First, unfurl the benevolent eyes like small slits on dancing bells. Then, we implore you to gently widen them, resembling fully bloomed red lotuses. Only in this gradual unveiling can we acclimate to the intensity of your gaze."

Additionally, she beseeches Him as a collective devotee to temper the fiery, sun-like intensity of the gaze by blending it with the serene compassion of the moon.

"Unfurl your divine eyes like the petals of a lotus, slowly, with the gentle temperature of the moon and the fiery sun.

Turn your gaze upon us. With your divine grace, all our mortal sorrows will completely dissipate."

With poetic eloquence, she captures our spiritual thirst.

As a drum, I have delivered beats for various dancers. The rows of bells they wear near their feet jingle with every rhythmic beat in the most enchanting way. The round metal bell, called a *Kinkini*, has a narrow slit in the middle. The dancer's anklet has multiple bells that jingle with each step.

The girls are poised for the spiritual union. Initially, the poet appeals to the mighty for divine regard upon devotees, likening it to eyes resembling narrow slits on dancing bells. Subsequently, they implore Him to magnify this glory until His eyes resemble fully bloomed lotuses. Concurrently, the poet requests moderation in the temperature of that intense gaze. As the divine eyes gradually expand, she implores to temper the brilliant gaze of a thousand suns with the soothing touch of the moon. The devotees revel in the profound vision without being overwhelmed. The girls wholeheartedly embrace the prospect of spiritual union. However, merging with Him will be a delicate process, as He exists on a different plane from their simple selves.

The devotees conclude the verse with a plea for the divine eyes to dispel all sorrows in this world. Will such earnest entreaties move Him?

DAY 23

Mari Malai Muzhanjil

Inside the Mountain Cave During Rains

We've journeyed from afar, armed with questions, our confidence unwavering. It is with a sense of entitlement, earned through devotion, that we seek complete communion with the divine spirit. Stripping away all traces of ego, we stand open, receptive and prepared to rouse Him from His divine repose.

Yet, a perplexing sense of reluctance seems to linger in the Lord, a hesitancy to unite with His ardent devotees. Is He akin to a hibernating lion, unwilling to emerge, and meet us? Questions persist—have we done enough, or is there more to be done?

The poet paints vivid imagery, echoing the devotees' spiritual yearning.

"In the dark recesses of the mountain cave, the majestic lion rests with its mate, during the wet, and rainy season. You, O Lord, embody such resplendent majesty! Come forth from this divine hibernation for the sake of your eager devotees.

Greet us with your wide-open, brilliant eyes, emanating both fiery protection, and the gentleness of red flower petals.

Arise, stretch, and claim your surroundings! We yearn to witness your regal splendor.

You are like the awe-inspiring lion, its magnificent mane swaying side-by-side. As the hair bristles and crackles, the splendid one resoundingly roars. Today, we aspire to witness this leonine facet in all its glory.

O Enchanter, with the violet hue of the Kayampoo flower! Grace us by emerging from your royal chamber. Walk towards us like the stately lion, bless us with the vision of your majestic gait as you ascend a grandly decorated throne, fitting for one as resplendent as you. Acknowledge our presence at your feet, inquire why we stand before you."

The devotees implore Him for protection, seeking refuge in the splendorous gaze of His eyes. These very eyes, when turned towards them, will soften with tenderness akin to the petals of a red flower. Their plea is for awareness, not hibernation, of their unwavering devotion.

Protection is sought not only from external enemies but also from internal foes —an insidious host of vices. As negativity is shed, the devotees blissfully align with the benevolent spirit.

Elevated in consciousness, they perceive His skin tone in the violet hue of the *Kayampoo* flower, imploring Him to awaken with the leonine majesty. The plea is clear—no slumber of disengagement. They beseech, like innocent children, seeking His *Vatsalya*, tender parental affection, for He is magnificent to all and formidable to adversaries.

Gathering like lion cubs seeking the gentle, protective parent, the devotees desire nothing more than the divine embrace.

DAY 24

Andru Ivulangam Alandan

The Day You Measured this World

Before Him, we stand as a united assembly, ready to articulate the sincerest intentions of our hearts. These young maidens, filled with gratitude, gather to extol His courage, protective decisions, and boundless compassion. In the echo of their voices and rhythmic beats, they express their unwavering devotion.

Overflowing with gratitude, they recount tales of His majestic deeds—tales of bravery, compassion, protectiveness, intelligence, love, and strength. Although the Omniscient needs no reminder, the act of acknowledging these virtues through our voices and beats becomes a sacred offering and a collective reminder to embrace those very qualities.

As we stand before Him, we acknowledge the One beyond the many avatars, transcending the limitations of time and space. Today, we comprehend the infinite dimensions of His being.

A drum, I may be, yet this verse envelops me in profound devotion. Its layers unfold like petals, and I pause to savor each word, carefully placed by the poet. In praising Him, we find ourselves immersed in the same love, seeking reasons to emulate His divine qualities and ascend to a sublime plane.

"We gather here to worship those praiseworthy feet that once measured this entire earth."

The tale of vanquishing ego and fostering generosity unfolds, referencing the Vamana Avatar, and the episode with King Mahabali.

"We laud the fame you won over Ravana, the southern king of Lanka."

The destructive war, fueled by Ravana's coveting of Sita, finds its place in this ode.

"We praise your courage in kicking Sakata, who came disguised as a hurtling cart, to smithereens."

The narrative of Krishna overcoming the ogre Sakata, sent by the jealous Kamsa, speaks of conquering natural enemies—rage, jealousy, and the desire to harm.

"You saw through ogres Vatsasura and Kapitasura, disguised as a calf, and a wood apple, respectively. Your wisdom destroyed them, serving as a slingshot against evil tendencies."

The poet references Krishna's compassion during storms, contrasting it with the deceitful ogres. The destruction of these ogres signifies the annihilation of negativity through wisdom, bravery, and righteousness.

"We worship your strength and intelligence in destroying both perpetrators simultaneously. As a protector, you lifted an entire mountain, using it as an umbrella to shelter us from the storm. We hail your compassion."

The Govardhan mountain episode becomes a symbol of divine compassion, illustrating that faith in the Divine can move mountains during life's storms.

"We hail the great spear in your victorious hand that removes hostility."

Hostile forces find solace in surrendering at His feet, transforming into worthy souls by relinquishing inimical desires.

"We come here to secure the gift of drums in submission, singing your praises perpetually. Please show your compassionate nature and emancipate us."

The flawless spirit of these young maidens shines as they seek access, juxtaposed with reformed enemies finding salvation. Will the Divine grant entrance to these blemish-free devotees?

In alluding to epics, the poet emphasizes the dharmic way of life. Stories like these resonate at various levels, inviting us to journey within, overcome negativity, and infuse our everyday lives with righteousness.

Who was Sakatasura?

In a bygone era, an ogre cleverly disguised as a cart sought to attack the infant Krishna. Krishna's mother, trusting the cart's safety, placed his basket within it. When the ogre attempted to strike, Krishna, with a single mighty kick, shattered the seemingly formidable cart to pieces.

The ogre in the form of a cart serves as a metaphor for the unnecessary baggage we often choose to carry in our lives. The malevolent jealousy embodied by Kamsa is the true ogre, while the contents of the cart represent negative burdens like lethargy, vanity, and hate.

Vatsasura, another demon, took the guise of a defenseless calf, symbolizing deceit, greed, and malicious intent. It serves as a reminder of the proverbial wolf in sheep's clothing. Dharma, the righteous path, replaces these destructive tendencies with love, devotion, humility, and service to all sentient and unfeeling beings. This narrative stands as a beacon, inspiring devotees to confront obstacles with love and compassion, doubling their karma.

In every epoch, unfairness, tyranny, disasters, and malevolence afflict the innocent. Devotion and adherence to dharma act as heroic forces, protecting against hostile influences. Overcoming evil is possible by relying on the divine and embodying courage, compassion, forgiveness, and dharmic principles.

The question arises: *Is submission a weakness*? The verse clarifies that submission to a higher plane is self-respect, while ego, claiming uniqueness, fosters self-importance. Submission unites, while ego divides.

Discernment is inherent in submission. Submitting to divine love is strength while bowing to bullies is not true submission. Submitting to courage fosters valor and builds fortitude. Submission is not groveling. One can understand submission better by contrasting it with groveling.

Submission carries a positive connotation. It is a more balanced and respectful act of yielding to authority or circumstances, or in the case of spiritual submission, it is yielding to the highest power. Groveling involves a more desperate and often demeaning attempt to seek approval or favor. The key distinction lies in the degree of respect, voluntariness, and dignity associated with each behavior.

DAY 25

Oruthimaganai Piranthu

Born to One Mother

The resplendent Lord rests majestically upon his adorned throne, poised to hear the earnest petitions of his devoted followers. Brimming with love, the devotees collectively acknowledge his transcendence beyond the cycles of birth and death, joyously celebrating his divine manifestation as Krishna.

In the eloquent words of Nammazhwar, he is *"Pirantha Maaya,"* the supreme illusionist who, in a profound act of self-birth, chose to manifest amidst cowherds as a devoted child. Even from the watchful eyes of mother Yashoda, he concealed his divine glories, playfully growing up as a mischievous youngster. These narratives, though seemingly simple, serve to unravel the complexities of profound phenomena.

Much like clinical scientists grappling with the enigma of the chicken and the egg, the devotees are confronted with the mystery of existence, prompting an ongoing quest for understanding.

Within this verse, there emerges a profound acknowledgment of the Lord's magnificence, coupled with gratitude for his accessible form as Krishna, fostering a sense of interconnectedness. The devotees recognize their participation in something profoundly meaningful, imploring the Lord to alleviate the sorrows born of separation from the Divine.

A subtle paradigm shift unfolds, resonating even in the altered cadence of my drumbeats. While initially dedicated to the pursuit of Oneness, a broader expansion beyond their microcosm becomes apparent. A sudden intuition prompts me to hoarsely ponder, "Could it be?"

Is it plausible that the Lord seeks to unite with us?

The timeless verse commences with the backstory of Krishna's birth, detailing the malevolent intentions of Kamsa, who coveted the throne, power, and life that Krishna embodied. Born to Devaki and Vasudha, Krishna was hidden, and raised by the loving Yashoda, thwarting Kamsa's relentless attempts at destruction. The demise of Kamsa ultimately resulted from his own malicious pursuits.

The devotees, singing of separation from the Divine, empathize with the gaze Krishna experienced when parted from his parents. This shared pain of separation prompts contemplation on whether the Lord endures a similar emotional struggle.

"You were born to Devaki but became Yashoda's son on the very night of your birth. Growing up in concealment, Kamsa's malevolence couldn't tolerate your existence. Your mere presence ignited jealousy in him, leading to harmful actions. Yet, you triumphed over his wicked schemes.

Oh, Lord! We, your devoted followers, beseech union with your divine spirit. We will beat the drum, singing your praises to your divine Consort. Gratefully, we'll recall the myriad ways you protect us, extol your abundance, and celebrate your valor. Through this, our separation sorrows will dissipate, and we shall rejoice together."

Once again, the word ***"Parai"*** resounds. The material drum transforms into a symbolic covenant, signifying the devotees' selfless surrender to the Lord's boundless love.

The analogy of Kamsa embodies the adharma or wrongful path. After all, Karma is neutral. Could aligning with adharma reduce the effulgence of the Supreme? The devotees suddenly perceive a novel insight – *separation pain is mutual*. Even the Supreme seeks unity, feeling recharged as divinity amplifies in creation.

In this verse, the request for a *Parai* transcends a mere drum; it symbolizes seeking the Lord's acceptance for enduring unity. "Rejoicing together" takes on a profound significance. The Lord, far from presiding in an echo chamber of praise, exemplifies humility, blurring the lines between protector and protected, giver, and receiver. He declares, "Look within. The Divine resides within you."

While many search externally for meaning, the true quest begins from within.

DAY 26

Male Manivanna!

Oh Sapphire-Hued Dear!

Today unfolds with a distinct aura, a whisper in hushed tones – *"Samyapathi."*

A subtle calibration lingers in the air, prompting contemplation on the delicate balance sought on the scales of existence.

Rolling the word *"Samyapathi"* in my heart, I savor its profound essence – the Lord as the Equalizer.

The depth of His love mirrors our collective faith, as He assumes the role of the Equal. While most devotees remain oblivious to this subtle shift, they earnestly engage with Him.

Now fully attuned, the Supreme seeks to understand the actions of His devotees. He wishes to grasp their desires and the motives that drive them, almost amused by the simplicity of their requests. In this seemingly effortless conversation, I observe eager devotees taking turns in asking, clarifying, and responding.

It's a sight to marvel at. Not everyone is born into spirituality. The girls, initially following the footsteps of their elders, now realize that devotion and purity are the essence of any faith. Guided by dharma in their formative years, they now regulate themselves with Him as their guiding light.

Commencing with praises of the spirit's greatness and lauding His complexion as *Manivanna*, the bluest sapphire, they convey the idea of infiniteness. Anything immeasurable, like the vast skies, and deep oceans, is rendered blue. The priceless gem in uninformed hands is but a mere pebble, and the girls now recognize the significance of divinity.

"O Beloved, adorned in brilliant sapphire hue! Throughout this holy month of Margazhi, we earnestly perform the penance of our elders. This simple act is our way to draw closer to you.

When asked about our desires, we seek milky-white conches akin to the Panchajanyam you blow. Let their sound resonate, filling the universe with your greatness.

Grant us colossal drums that echo your name, accompanied by myriad devoted voices praying for your eternity. Bright oil lamps for spiritual illumination, flags symbolizing unity with you, and a vast canopy to celebrate our harmony.

Supreme Lord, the infant on a banyan leaf, grace us with your divine presence as we conclude our celebration singing your praise."

He seems pleased with their verse, yet feigns a quizzical stance. If they desire divine unity, why do they request material things?

Returning to their original plea, *"Supreme Lord, the infant on a banyan leaf, grace us with your divine presence as we conclude our celebration singing your praise."*

The milky-white conches resound, proclaiming His greatness. The giant drums beat to the melodies of devoted singers, celebrating His eternity. Bright lamps symbolize spiritual awakening under His canopy adorned with flags and festoons, emblems reflecting Him.

In response, the damsels earnestly declare, "As we celebrate your majesty, we fervently pray for your perpetuity."

Perpetuity, they say. But if the Lord is indestructible, why is there a need for perpetuity?

Could it be that He needs them as much as they need Him?

The poet beautifully explores the dynamics of devotion and the divine through vivid imagery and metaphorical storytelling. The devotees, armed with pure love, approach the Supreme with rituals passed down through generations, guided by the wisdom of gurus and elders. The reference to "Baby on the Banyan Leaf" carries profound significance, portraying an innocent image that conceals disarmament, trust, and accessibility. The divine reciprocates the pure love of devotees by taking the form of a baby Krishna on a banyan leaf, symbolizing the approachability, and humility of the limitless Supreme. The seemingly calm waters represent Pralaya, the great deluge, with the potential to engulf everything. Yet, even in His sleep, He remains conscious in *Yoga Nidra*, or dynamic sleep. There is deep trust-binding relaxation with the fullest awareness.

The seemingly contradictory nature of this portrayal underscores the essence of devotion and purity, irrespective of the chosen approach. The Magnificent descends to the level of innocent devotees, embodying the vulnerability, and openness represented by the baby on the banyan leaf. The devotees, in turn, play the nurturing role of mothers, reminiscent of Yashoda caring for baby Krishna. The poet draws a poignant parallel to the story of Krishna revealing vast cosmic expanses within His tiny mouth, symbolizing the boundless nature of the divine within the confines of apparent childlike simplicity.

The image of the devotees feeling like protective mothers to the divine, while overlooking His limitlessness in their eagerness to shield, adds layers to the exploration of the devotee-deity relationship. The poet invites readers to imagine the profound surprise of discovering the rarity of divine greatness, akin to holding what was thought to be a simple pebble only to realize it's the rarest sapphire. This vivid analogy magnifies the preciousness of the divine treasure held tightly by the devotees.

The journey persists as the devotees unravel the identity of the master magician, emphasizing the continuous exploration, and discovery of the divine essence. The verses beautifully capture the interplay of love, innocence, devotion, and the infinite nature of the divine, inviting readers to reflect on the profound dynamics between the devotee and the Supreme.

DAY 27

Koodarai Vellum

The One who Wins over Hostile Foes

As the vow approaches its culmination, I've journeyed alongside this dedicated group. From the austere beginnings of the initial verses, we've delved deeper into the spiritual realms.

"Oh, Govinda, Conqueror of enemies! Our sole aspiration is You! You are our highest reward, and thus we gather here to exalt with drums in celebration. In doing so, we seek the gifts from You, praised by the entire world. We'll adorn ourselves with bracelets, shoulder ornaments, earrings, and their graceful accessories. Anklets, resplendent clothing, a feast of rich milk and sweet rice – all to overflow with buttery richness beyond our elbows. Stay united with us in this joyous feast, where we blissfully wear the gifts and revel in Your abundance."

Something extraordinary is unfolding, and its resonance is profound. From the initial days of austerity, the damsels have evolved, shedding cosmetic aids, and perfumed accessories on the second day, for these would not align with their devotion. Waiting in the cold for Him, they now embrace joy, celebrating their adornment. Spiritual alchemy turns material joys into divine bliss.

In my perspective, we've acquired something in this newfound proximity that we lacked before. We shape our world, and the path, once simple, often gets obscured by personal desires, creating an obstacle course. To reach this point, we've surmounted internal, and external hurdles.

In this present moment, the Lord stands fully accessible before us. Overwhelmed with bliss, the guru perceives, while the girls may not easily grasp that the Lord is testing and teasing them. Superficially, this may seem like a simple verse, but its spiritually profound layers reveal themselves.

The girls persist in seeking acceptance from Him, addressing Him as the conqueror of enemies. Yet, He has not fully accepted this group of women who approach with pure love.

Unbeknownst to them, they are beginning to radiate His effulgence. Another revelation strikes me – the girls mirror the divine qualities and are not separate from the Divine, even if they cannot yet perceive it.

With pure innocence, they question the Magician, the one who effortlessly triumphs over enemies and unites humanity. Why does it have to be so challenging for Him to win and gather friends who willingly come to Him with love?

With familiarity, they claim the rewards earned through their journey – brilliant ornaments like anklets, bracelets, upper arm ornaments, earrings, and new clothing, all culminating in a feast featuring the sweet dessert *Akaaravadisal*.

The poet strategically places these material elements with intent. These ornaments and articles illustrate the rapture felt in celebrating union with the divine spirit through everyday objects.

It's challenging to articulate this unique feeling. Just as various names are ascribed to the divine, the spirit understands mortal limitations. Through the material, the poet carves a path to the spirit. Incorporating it into the daily transforms joy into bliss.

Anklets signify the foundation or feet. Starting from there, each piece of jewelry represents the adornment of the higher senses. Wrapped in the fabric of devotion, the devotees nourish their souls with the sweetest ambrosia of divinity. Their bliss flows like clarified butter with the union or spiritual acceptance.

The joys of the concrete realm are but one layer. It's now time for rapture, abundance, and jubilant celebrations. The poet captures this abstract spiritual sentiment of uniting with the divine spirit through concrete examples.

Revisiting the second verse of Andal's suite of thirty, the initial vow indicated abstinence from cosmetic aids and rich food during the early stages of the journey. This abstinence symbolizes the suffering felt without the spirit within. Now, the girls comprehend that abstaining from feasting was due to separation from the Divine. No worldly pleasure can fulfill a soul devoid of spirituality.

In this verse, a celebration for all senses is envisioned. When close to the Divine, there's no holding back. Rewards come in the form of dazzling ornaments, fine clothing, and rich food. As divinity answers their call, devotees revel in infinite abundance. The extended fasting symbolizes their test of overcoming obstacles to reach Him. Now, the union feels like a lavish feast. The image of clarified butter coursing down their elbows during the sweet feast signifies the profound feelings of devotion resulting from this union.

A shifting power dynamic becomes apparent. Until this moment, the devotees were striving to reach Him. He, now, is fully engaged, and accessible to them. The imagery of the Lord serving devotees unveils another facet of the One – Nirankari, the One without ego.

The emphasis on living without malice, ego, or hatred from within, and without is interwoven. Amicability, unity, and collective strength lead to abundance, joy, and true bliss when every creature prospers. Devotees may be at different points on the spiritual path, but when those in the worldly realm fulfill their duties with dharma and devotion, it results in grateful abundance for all. For those who have transcended material bonds, abundance is found in spiritual proximity and union. They feel adorned and decorated.

The devotees now respect and revere themselves more, recognizing themselves as minute particles of the Divine. Adorning oneself is not vain or egotistic; it's a celebration of union with the Highest. Viewing themselves in the highest regard as part of the Supreme, they are *jivatmas*, or individual souls, whose bodies, minds, and souls are divine gifts. With this knowledge, they begin to surrender themselves in utmost reverence to the *Paramatma* or the Infinite Soul.

DAY 28

Karavaigal Pinnsendru

Following the Herd

Satisfied with their responses, the playful probing continues. "You assert that all you need is complete and loving surrender. So why engage in vows and rituals? I'm curious. What is the end goal?"

Whether they address the awe-inspiring Narayana, the Supreme Enlightened One, or Mukunda, the bestower of Moksha, or salvation, He questions like the simple Govinda—the sublime cowherd, sharing a kinship that transcends the complexities of divine titles. In the essence of Govinda, the divine is not distant or shrouded in grandeur; rather, it's an intimate connection, reminiscent of a tender kinship found in the simplicity of a shared pastoral life. In each name, He resonates with a familiarity that invites a profound closeness, a recognition that the Supreme is not just an abstract concept but a companion on the shared journey of existence. Whether acknowledging His supreme wisdom, His role as a bestower of salvation or simply embracing Him as Govinda, the heart of the connection remains grounded in the beauty of simplicity and shared camaraderie.

"You are a wellspring of knowledge, a guru, a seer, a Jnani, and yet, to us, you are the kindred Govinda, the sublime cowherd."

Drawing from their lineage of cowherds, they emphasize the enduring connection—both blood and spiritual—that will never break with this verse.

"O Lord, we are simple folk who know nothing beyond following our grazing cows in the forest to sustain ourselves. While ignorant of the enlightened perspectives on understanding the infinite facets of your supreme nature, we cowherds only know this blessing. Therefore, we will leverage our kinship, linking us perpetually with you. O Flawless One, Leader of Cowherds (Govinda!), we will never sever this relationship with you. In our familiarity, we've played and loved you like one of us. In our ignorance, we overlooked your greatness and addressed you in the singular. Please forgive us, and do not mistake this purest love for disrespect. O Lord and Master, we seek the divine acceptance of our surrender to you."

In their contemplation, a sudden realization of entitlement dawns upon them. Have they unintentionally taken this relationship for granted? Amid their playfulness, banter, and the purest of love stemming from this kinship, they might have addressed Him in the singular. As an act of pure love, they seek forgiveness for this transgression.

From being the Supreme Being Narayana, distant in the initial verses, He has become accessible as Govinda through the unalloyed love of His devotees. The seers, they acknowledge, had mentioned this quality in the Lord. In the state of *Saulabhya*, the Lord is fully accessible to devotees who come to Him in trusting surrender or *Prapanna*.

This verse underscores the linkage and interdependence that emanate from such devotion. The poet echoes the idea that despite memorizing spiritual texts, understanding them, and engaging in learning, and debates, the Supreme is best attained when a righteous devotee opens their heart and soul to receive divinity.

The young damsels portray themselves as limited beings, earnestly following their elders to reach the Supreme Self. They question whether He would not accept them in their simplicity, acknowledging the rites, and rituals created by devotees with love and devotion to fathom the complexity.

The devotees realize the multifaceted and supreme nature of the divine. They extend a heartfelt apology if they ever overlooked His greatness or addressed Him in the singular. They are quick to clarify that their familiarity was rooted in the purest of love and not disrespect. They yearn for the divine acceptance of their surrender.

Unaware that they have already attained *saulabhya*, full accessibility through pure love, they contrast their perceived lowliness with supreme loftiness. In the Lord's weighing scale, their devotion equals His supremacy, erasing any differences.

The girls, without delving into complex texts of Vedas, Upanishads, science, philosophy, or religion, start comprehending the Supreme through loving action. They acknowledge the apparent contradiction between vast texts attempting to encapsulate Narayana's infinitude and their own understanding through the sweetness of Krishna's form. Their minds delve inward to find supreme bliss, meditating with pure love to realize the spirit in every fiber. In the moment of *"Ikshana,"* the devotee witnesses the infinite creativity of the Birthless One, realizing the Formless, or *Nirguna*.

Chapter 14

Segment E

DAY 29

Sitram Sirukale

In the Wee Hours of Dawn

Before us lies an array of drums, each resonating with newfound devotion, even the smallest ones. Striking these drums brings immense joy to both the drummer and the audience. The drums themselves exhibit a variety of shapes and sizes, some with peculiar forms, others adorned with bells, and beads.

With a sweeping gesture, he declares, "There! You have what you asked for!"

But why does he choose to playfully tease?

Unfazed, the devotees inquire, "Is this truly how you perceive our intent?"

With heartfelt devotion, they sing this verse:

"Oh, Govinda! In the cold, early morning hours, we come to you, desiring only to worship at your golden lotus-like feet. Born into the community of innocent cowherds, like us, you, Govinda, cannot

abandon us due to that kinship alone. Allow us to serve you in devotion. All we ask is for you to accept our humble offerings.

Look here, you comprehend everything. Yet, why do you seem to overlook this simple fact? We seek not just your grace or word (parai) for this day alone but for generations and perpetuity. Only you can erase any attachment to material attachments. Our sole aim is to worship you, to be guided by you. We yearn to remain united with you for posterity."

Now, it's time they articulate their intent to Him through their voices. While he may have teased it out playfully, they now reveal their purpose with earnestness.

Why did they embark on this vow?

At its core, it revolves around the principles of *dharma*, their birth, and the natural law, or *Hrta*. *Dharma*, in its most tangible definition, encompasses proper conduct, a guiding code for navigating life. Amidst the attachments, bonds, possessions, perceived gains, and losses, joys, sorrows, and emotions that make up their existence, they recognize these as mere snapshots that, when allowed, can overshadow the entirety of their story.

Purushartas, the four desires pursued with mindful intent for the soul, encapsulate the core aspirations of *Dharma*, *Artha*, *Kama*, and *Moksha*. Woven with the divine, these desires infuse the present with depth, richness, and purpose.

Dharma, the ethical warp, and weft, upholds righteous, and moral actions in harmony with the natural law or Hrta. It is the guiding principle for leading a contented life.

Artha encompasses material wealth, comforts, and welfare, aiding survival, and prosperity.

Kama involves desire, enjoyment, delight, sensual satisfaction, and love for family, friends, and the universe.

Moksha is the spiritual realization that unveils a greater purpose in life, fostering a connection to the divine.

United with the right action according to the natural law (*Hrta*), these desires foster coexistence, and prosperity for humans and the entire universe.

Rta or *Hrta*, an ethical principle in Vedic texts, features set ordinances for beings to follow, forming a part of dharmic life. Failure to adhere to *Hrta* principles was perceived as a cause of suffering, aligning with the concept of Karma. The physical manifestations of *Hrta* include elements like water, rain, and the sun, while its moral order lies in truth, serving as the basis for *Dharma* and the resulting *Karma*.

The Tiruppavai verses progress from the realm of cowherd lasses, offering prayers for abundance, unity, positive thoughts, protection, and righteous living. The girls learn to overcome personal obstacles and acknowledge the benevolence and generosity of the Supreme throughout their journey. As they pray for perpetuity, a sense of reciprocity emerges, emphasizing the symbiotic relationship between the divine and the devotees.

In their quest for the deity with a thousand names, the girls recognize that their needs make the divine appear in various forms. Through dharmic acts, they understand the divine as both singular and manifold, transcending the limitations of the material world.

The verses convey the impermanence of the body and the mystery surrounding the individual soul. While religion can't fully explain it, science continues its exploration. Incorporating dharma and spirituality transforms each moment, providing meaning to life.

The journey, as interpreted by the guru, serves as a roadmap for life stages. The earlier verses emphasize collective prayers, grounding individuals, and fostering serenity. Slowly, the spiritual connection becomes the sole attachment that gives meaning, dimension, and depth to all other needs.

Life and death, perceived as points in an uncharted continuum, prompt contemplation on the impermanence of worldly attachments. The unperishable energy of the soul raises questions about its fate after the body perishes. Incorporating spirituality into a daily life of abundance while adhering to dharma becomes the essence of the journey.

Moksha, or salvation, emerges as a reasonable means and end, offering a path to find purposeful bliss. Awareness of the divine early in life enables the individual to lead a respectful existence within the larger universe. The journey unfolds through moments of prayer, gratitude, and the acknowledgment of the divine's role in providing strength and guidance.

The poetic journey encapsulates the significance of the vow and the evolving understanding of the divine, transitioning from the provider role to the destination. The drum, or *parai*, assumes different meanings throughout the journey— representing generosity, the divine word, and victorious surrender.

The progression from addressing Narayana to embracing Govinda reflects the girls' evolving divine consciousness.

The journey is a step by step realization, culminating in the understanding that the divine resides within them through kindness, respect, compassion, courage, fairness, benevolence, gratitude, charity, reciprocity, and unalloyed love.

The Tiruppavai verses mirror the sojourn, illustrating that in reaching the divine, both the divine and the goal are equal. The early verses showcase the girls navigating habits, attitudes, and perceptions, eventually realizing the impermanence of material possessions and attachments. Connecting the individual soul to the Greater Soul adds layers of meaning, texture, and bliss to daily life. The desire for unity with the divine, *"Yetraikkum yezh yezh piravikkum undanodu,"* emphasizes a timeless yearning for perpetual union.

The guru, although not a devoted maiden undertaking the vow, becomes part of the journey through the beating of the thirty verses. The exploration of the word *"Parai"* signifies a multifaceted journey, awakening inner divinity, and recognizing the divine as both singular and manifold.

As the girls seek the divine, the yearning to merge with the spirit grows. Through sincere efforts, they realize that they possess the spiritual keys to obtain full access and beyond. The truth lies in recognizing that whoever lives within us ultimately determines our identity. The Tiruppavai verses encapsulate this profound journey, transforming ordinary moments into sublime experiences and offering a roadmap for a rich, soulful life.

DAY 30

Vanga Kadal

Ship-laden Ocean

"We extol Madhava, the Devotee of Lakshmi, who embraced the goddess close to his heart. He, bearing the names Keshava and Krishna, churned up the milky ocean laden with ships to obtain the immortal ambrosia. The maidens have fulfilled their vow, their divine radiance mirroring the glow of the moon. In Brindavan, they fervently prayed, worshiped, and pledged themselves to the Lord for the coveted Parai (drum, word, submission). The captivating tale of acquiring the Parai is narrated in verses by the daughter of Bhattar Piran, adorned with a tulasi bead and a lotus necklace.

The awe-inspiring Lord stands tall, his broad shoulders resembling mountains. His magnetic red eyes and sacred countenance exude majestic splendor. As devotees earnestly comprehend and recite these 30 Tamil verses, they shall receive the benevolent grace and attain eternal bliss."

On the final day, resonating with divine rhythm through the thirtieth verse, a profound state of consciousness unfolds. Is this yet another layer distinct from waking, sleep, and dreaming? Within this clarity emerges an awareness that we all reside within the Divine, and the Divine resides within us. The same word *Parai*, in this context, symbolizes the ultimate, victorious surrender to the Supreme.

The final verse is a hymn of praise to Lord Vishnu, now harmoniously merged with his divine consort, Lakshmi. The devoted maidens, having successfully completed their vow, have reached the Absolute. The verse holds significance for those at various stages of divinity, transitioning from the concrete to the abstract.

Expressing gratitude, the poet acknowledges herself as Bhattarpiran's daughter, adorned with a tulasi bead necklace symbolizing the absolute unity of Vishnu and Lakshmi. Bhattarpiran is the actual name of the priest, but due to his mind which is fixated on Vishnu, he is referred to as Vishnuchitta as well.

Why does she identify as the daughter of Bhattarpiran when united with the Self? When the Divine accepts the individual, respect for the devotee arises. Tied to the worldly existence, she pays homage to the elder who initiated her into sacred texts and sparked the inquiry into divinity. Bhattarpiran, her father, expresses devotion by weaving garlands for the Lord, and she offers her verses with the same spirit. It is a grateful dedication to another devotee.

The unlettered damsels may not grasp the scriptures intricately, but the poet imparts the purest essence through these verses. Recited with love and devotion, divine grace showers as health, wealth, and prosperity, enriching the universe. The universe thrives under the benevolence of the Divine, and Lakshmi, the goddess of abundance, is integral to this completeness.

Does surrender to the Absolute equate to defeat of oneself? Is merging with the Divine a loss of individuality? The Supreme is a benevolent benefactor, and recognizing gifts with love and gratitude feels like overflowing ghee from a sweet dish. Respecting the cosmic unity through sharing abundance and acknowledging interdependence brings bliss. The individual, devoid of the Spirit, becomes forgotten, unhappy, and egotistic when worldly symbols fade. Recognizing individuality in the Self and the Self in the individual defines unity, yielding unique, and powerful gains.

The Mundaka Upanishad's allegory of two golden birds mirrors the journey of the girls. Initially attached to ego-driven desires like the bird sitting on lower branches observing only its small world, bird, the journey is a progression towards the unitive state with the Supreme Self, akin to the bird sitting on the higher branches with a panoramic view of everything it beholds. The girls' recognition of their interconnectedness with the macrocosm reflects the bliss of unison and gratitude.

Observing the young women transition from the concrete to the abstract in their faith feels like a different life with the acknowledgment of the Divine. While individuals change, grow, and sometimes regress, the choice to elevate oneself persists. The desire expressed by the girls to remain close to the Supreme in perpetuity resonates deeply. Identifying qualities like kindness, compassion, empathy, and generosity as attributes of the Supreme reflects the kinship referred to by the girls.

Interpreting Narayana (or the Supreme as one chooses to call) not merely as an avatar but as the source of the eternal and unchangeable, the devotees realize divine grace is attained through virtuous practices. The poet's verses plant seeds for a spiritual forest, replacing harmful thoughts with kind ones.

The journey involves knocking on different doors, beating upon various drums, and awakening spirituality. The Divine transitions from being the Provider to the Destination. The drum, or *Parai*, symbolizes generosity, the divine word, and victorious surrender. The unlettered damsels, once attached to temporary, and external pursuits, shed ego to understand the true nature of self and seek salvation through selfless surrender.

The journey begins as a bridal vow, reflecting the quest to find the inner core. Progressing from a focus on the external and temporary to discerning and identifying with an unchanging, steady core, the girls undergo a transformative journey. The poet does not disparage material gifts; instead, she advocates gratitude and perpetuity for plentifulness, infusing daily life with spiritual essence.

Identifying with impermanent attributes can lead to misery, disappointment, and suffering. The tranquil mind arises when recognizing the imperishable, unchanging core amidst the fleeting objects. The girls' journey, initially perceived as a quest to acquire drums, evolves in perception from start to finish, reflecting a profound shift in identification.

How Does One Understand the Self?

The unlettered lasses enjoy life and its gifts in a dharmic fashion. Yet, like cows, they seek direction from the cowherd to lead them home. They search for the greater self in innocent, familiar ways. The need to merge with the Supreme is a quest to find the inner independent self.

Vedas and Upanishads speak about the self in detail. While they are complex and beautiful, most of us are not blessed to understand the content from the get-go. Most humans are drawn to concrete explanations first, and some move on to abstractions. These texts have inspired several saints to simplify them, and the concept of Bhakti, or pure devotion, often forms the core of their teachings.

When there is a tranquil union with the self, a soul is undisturbed, serene, beyond sin and sorrow, and has attained its purpose.

Chapter 15

Surrender: A Celebration of Spiritual Enrichment

Does surrender to the Absolute mean the defeat of oneself? When we merge with the divine, are we losing our individuality?

The Supreme is a benefactor. As Andal beautifully articulates in her *Kudarai Vellum* verse, the love and gratitude in recognizing these gifts feel like the overflowing ghee covering their elbows from the sweet dish in their hands. This partaking of offerings in the forms of grain, sweet cane, butter, milk, the giving cows, ornaments, and clothing are all aspects of the universe. Sharing abundance, removing adverse feelings, and the cognizance of interdependence with resulting gratitude are aspects of respecting the cosmic unity of which one is a part. It sometimes feels like this recognition is surrender when one falls in line with this order. The individual without the spirit often is unfulfilled. When temporary symbols of prestige, wealth, beauty, social status, and vanity accouterments fall off, all that is left is a disturbed soul and deep spiritual hunger.

The thirty-day verses are like the first steps that take the devotees as far as they want. The kernel of understanding the spirit lies within these thirty. These questions were on my mind, as well as others, as we began the quest. These verses are seeds, and with love, one can grow a plant, garden, or forest of spirituality.

Who is a devotee? A devotee is someone who loves the Absolute. In the Bhagavad Gita, Krishna quotes the idea that a true devotee sees the Supreme soul as the soul in all living beings. The Supreme Being resides in himself equally everywhere. Therefore, the devotees are undoubtedly part of the Supreme, and divine consciousness comes with a complete surrender of ego. When the devotee loves the Supreme, then there is a manifestation of the Supreme. The Absolute manifests itself the way the devotees see. To the young brides, He is the eternal bridegroom. To the ones who love the Supreme like a child, the manifestation is that of a child. As for the undevoted or the ones who do not want to see the Absolute, there is no manifestation. It is easy to augment the Supreme within one through love, service, and surrender of ego.

Is there a method to transform self-love into becoming a devotee? Dispensing service to all sentient creatures, including oneself with dharma, is the way. We constantly make choices that affect the web of life. An alternative exists in how we use our senses and organs to act. It could be a small service like showing kindness to someone that offers a moment of greatness. Our mind perceives this action; while doing so, ego takes precedence over other facets of the mind. A devotee needs to act like a sentry, push out their ego, and acknowledge with gratitude that the God within has enabled this service. When we begin to think we are indispensable, we let ego creep in and forget to connect with the divine. Similarly, accepting the grace that comes our way is a way of revering the self within. We can dispense the same to others through understanding if we love ourselves.

Is the Supreme dependent on His devotees? The Supreme simply is. The unison with the divine produces a feeling of bliss in the devotee. Yet, humility exists in the Absolute when there is the divine manifestation of a loving devotee. A wise guru from another century named Raidas provides an analogy to the relationship between the Absolute and the devotee to a unique fragrance in gold (sonhe me suhaga). Losing oneself to the divine brings an extra gain unlike any other. If He's the flame, then the devotee is the wick. Together, they express the light burning night and day. The conjoined Supreme and the devotee are unable to tell apart.

Why are there so many names and gods if the Supreme is One?

The Supreme is sufficient. There is no limitation, boundary, or "boxing" with the One. However, creatures are limited. Even a seemingly insurmountable task is easy if one breaks it down into parts. So it is, in understanding the Infinite. We use our five senses to understand the Formless One. Vibrating chants lift us higher; we may use idols to see and feel the intangible. We may attribute names based on a single facet of the divine or use our noses to smell the fragrance in flowers, offering them to a favorite deity as a reminder of who put them there. We may use incense to associate or invoke the spirit through other senses. Lighting lamps dispel darkness. We prepare tasty offerings to recognize the one who put them there and who gave us the ability to create, share, and enjoy. These exercises are not for the Supreme but reminders for the beings. It provides a higher awareness and an opportunity to express gratitude for self. A simple example of providing fruit to the divine is a reminder of how that fruit got into one's hand. Sharing offerings with others connects individuals by sparking compassion. Senses, mind, and intellect bind us.

The Shukla Yajurveda 32.3 quotes, "*Na Tasya Pratima Asti,*" while referring to the spirit. Pratima, at a concrete level, means image in Sanskrit. The literal meaning of the sentence limits when translated as "There's no image like the One." The deeper meaning of Pratima is unparalleled. The symbolic meaning, therefore, would be that there is no equivalent to God. That being the case, through limited senses and intellect, one views the divine as images, icons, and idols. There is room for that interpretation as well. How else would one comprehend the incomprehensible without baby steps? These are merely ways to understand the Formless One. One can ignite devotion with both means. By repetition, one may realize that there is something else beyond the five senses that goes beyond beliefs to another domain: the realm of experiencing divinity. From crawling to holding support and walking, the baby learns to walk and run. Accepting these stages as part of evolution is the key. When one is stuck on rituals, rites, idols, and religion, the next stage is finding the divine remains undiscovered.

In this journey, the Supreme is given a masculine gender. Is there a categorization?

Categorization comes naturally for mortals. It's easier to break down and hold a facet of the Infinite rather than understand the Unmanifested. Sanskrit grammar ascribes feminine gender to certain words. For example, in chapter 10, verse 34, the Omnipresent represents speech among women as *Kirti* or glory, *Sri* or prosperity, *Vak* or speech, *Smriti* or memory, *Medha* or intelligence, *Dhriti* or fortitude, and as *Kshama, or* patience.

The Absolute manifests self as one or all qualities in people. The Shakti tradition views the Supreme as a woman.

Within the poet's narrative, the cowherd girls in the garden of Brindavan or Ayarpadi worship the Goddess Katyayani. The goddess defeated the evil demon Mahishasura. The male trinity: Brahma, Vishnu, and Shiva blessed her with the masculine energy of creation, preservation, and destruction to add to her infinite creativity.

Similarly, the mighty lord Srinivasa's name means that the goddess of compassion and abundance, Lakshmi, resides in his heart.

The Bhakti tradition holds one view that the relationship with the divine is that of lovers. Other traditions hand over an androgynous aspect to the Supreme.

When the female and male principles coexist inseparably, it is the unity of opposites in the universe.

Vishnu holds Lakshmi in his heart, where she establishes *Daya*, or compassion.

Ardhanarishvara, the lord half woman, is another name when Shiva and Shakti are conjoined. Shiva is the ascetic, and Shakti holds the mirror symbolizing the material or imaginary world.

Fusing spirituality and material parts erases opposing forces and brings about a nonduality. At certain moments, one power may be more dominant than the other. Still, when viewed over a long period, they work together to maintain equilibrium, harmony, and balance to prove that duality is not totality. Call it a balance of Yin and Yang in the universe. The color wheel demonstrates opposites are complementary. They're equal parts of a whole.

The Brahman or Absolute is nameless and formless. Seers sometimes used allegories to help transition from the concrete to the abstract. In some texts, Nayikas or females make up the mortal world, and the Supreme is the ultimate Purusha. The quest toward the divine is like a marriage or union. The poet Andal used bridal mysticism to lead her world to connect with the highest spirit.

If one took this concept further, when devotees mirror the Supreme, they have full access to become conjoined with divinity.

What Is Divine Bridal Romanticism?

When a devotee imagines herself as a lover of the lord with intense ardor, we have a version of bridal romanticism. In several cultural traditions, there are descriptions of this kind of devotion. Christian mystics write of becoming the "Bride of Christ" to demonstrate the intense love and passion for Lord Jesus. St. Teresa of Avila considered Him her divine husband and partner. She wrote the following verse from one of her songs,

"I am Thine and Born for Thee.
Take, O lord, my loving heart:
See, I yield it to Thee whole,
With my body, life, and soul
And my nature's every part.
Sweetest Spouse, my life Thou art.
I have given myself to Thee
What wilt has thou done with me?"

Communion with the divine in devotees is vital, and one of the ways is to approach it with the passion for union between the lover and his consort. Therefore, many male devotees have evoked the inner woman to ally with the lord.

Narasinh Mehta from Gujarat was an ardent devotee of Krishna. He sang about the joy of dancing like a woman, like a *Gopika*, or cowherd girl surrounding Krishna. So, he began to sing, and dance like her and experienced incomparable sweetness and bliss of union with the divine.

What is the Bridal Mysticism of Andal?

Although she comes equipped with spirituality, the true leader Andal recognizes that most people, not just in her generation but through centuries, will need to ignite their inner eye. With *Vinaya* or humility, she approaches the grand idea of leading the simple-thinking girls entangled in the material realm to incorporate spirituality into their daily lives. Her words resonate even today. She does not shy from a challenge. Instead, she chooses to work with it. Their simplicity is not an obstacle, nor is the material world in which they exist. The girls came from the cowherd family. Honoring their world lens, the poet ignites spirituality.

During the season of *Margazhi*, the lasses perform a seasonal marriage vow to secure an ideal spouse. Taking this idea, Andal leads them in divine thought, word, and deed to spiritual expansion.

The poet depicts experience with the Absolute as an irrevocable, loyal, loving, and selfless union between a harmonious couple in marriage.

The girls use familiar rituals within their microcosm to perform a marriage vow. She ties this tradition to the grander design of the divine quest. The idea of the ardent devotee's soul as that of a yearning bride alludes to the Absolute as the Eternal bridegroom.

There is an intense longing to unite with Him, as she asks the white conch the Divine Lover blows from in the poem in the Nachiyar Thirumozhi called, *Karpuram Naarumo, Kamala Poo Narumo?*

"Oh, white conch, you have the fortune of proximity to His beautiful coral-red lips. Tell me, how does the Brave One's lips taste? Does his fragrant breath feel tingly fragrant as camphor, or does it possess the cool fragrance of the lotus flower? Do his lips taste as sweet as rock candy? Do tell O fortunate one, for I yearn to experience this divine sweetness."

To Andal, the supreme is both the path and the destination. The individual on the divine way never gets lost, where surrender increases self-respect, and devotees are in synchronicity with the sacred.

The awareness of the insignificance of the individual and the shedding of the ego is a natural result. Humility is very different from humiliation. The perception of being part of the Grand Absolute brings a different kind of joy that supersedes petty, selfish absorption. Instead, this unity of loving, and being loved is much grander, sweeter, and more prosperous.

The seer Ramana Maharishi perceives this concept through the prism of unselfish love for the divine. "Where the love for God is for the sake of love alone, this love is not even for the sake of salvation..."

What is this ego, and why should it be shed? What happens when the ego is shed?

The ego is a sticky wicket. It resides in the fortress of the mind. A devotee recognizes that it is a shadow and not a fact. Only consciousness, the Absolute, can free individuals from the ego's net. The poet echoes the idea that none of the material enjoyment is eschewed. In fact, the spiritual dimension augments enjoyment with mindfulness, gratitude, charity, and empathy. The individual recognizes that this is a temporary world and enjoys it but with a difference. The ego is not supreme; it is the ego that enjoys the company of the higher power. The ego has a different shelf life than the spirit. The spirit lasts forever. The Absolute and the devotee are like the two golden birds on the *Pippala* tree. It is found in the Mundaka Upanishad, a philosophical text within the Vedic tradition, written by the sage Mundaka.

The Upanishad describes two birds sitting on the same tree. One bird is actively engaged in eating the fruits of the tree, representing the individual soul, or *Jivatman*. The fruits symbolize the experiences and consequences of one's actions in the material world. The *Jivatman* is frenetically entangled in acquisition, and consumption within the cycle of birth and death, experiencing the fruits of its karma.

The second bird, however, is simply watching without eating. This bird signifies the supreme consciousness, the *Paramatman* or the Higher Self. It remains a silent observer, unaffected by the actions, and experiences of the individual soul. It has a higher perch and sees all the drama below and beyond. It represents the eternal, unchanging aspect of reality beyond the transient world of phenomena.

Are they really two birds or one?

The teaching conveys the idea that the *Jivatman* and *Paramatman* are connected, just like the two birds on the same tree. While the individual soul is engrossed in the material world, the Higher Self remains a witness, untouched by worldly experiences. The aim is for the individual soul to recognize its divine nature, transcend the cycle of birth and death, and realize its oneness with the supreme consciousness.

What Ensues When One Clings to the Ego?

In the realm of Sanskrit, "*Aham*" signifies "I," and "*Kara*" translates to "anything created." This term, rooted in Vedic Philosophy, has permeated Hinduism, Buddhism, Sikhism, and Jainism. Intriguingly, all these religions advocate the shedding of individual ego. Loosely defined, Ahankara attributes concrete existence to the ego, rooted in subjective consciousness.

Within Hinduism, Ahamkara stands as one of the four components of the antahkarana or inner organ, alongside *Buddhi, Citta,* and *Manas*. Buddhi, derived from the Sanskrit "Budh," meaning to wake or discern, plays a role in distinguishing between the real and the illusory on the spiritual quest.

Citta, rooted in the word "*Cit*," meaning to think, represents pure awareness, or consciousness of the mind. It extends to encompass the universal consciousness and, in Pali texts, includes the emotive side of consciousness.

Manas, the concept of the mind as a holistic thinking faculty, involves a volition for action or inaction. Yet, for the self to truly be present, *Ahamkara*, or Ego must be relinquished. When the mind dwells in this state of ego, the concept of self becomes attached to external things—be they material, concrete, or ideational.

This attachment can manifest in various forms. For instance, someone might believe that material wealth, social status, or a particular idea makes them great. However, the pursuit of this perceived greatness often leaves the individual self perpetually dissatisfied.

When one clings fiercely to a concept, it becomes another form of attachment. Consider the example of a proponent of peace and non-violence who, when challenged, may find themselves resorting to violence. Such thoughts, illusory, and ego-driven, often deviate from the user's true character. The ego, with its identification of something small and impermanent, leads to human suffering.

Andal, through her poems, simplifies these age-old philosophical debates. The ego, she asserts, is divisive, and disrespectful, causing sorrow. Its annihilation, on the other hand, clears obstacles on the spiritual path. By pulverizing the ego and surrendering to divine grace, sorrows lose their impact, and pleasure attains the unalloyed purity of love.

The drama at the lower level of existence, with its cycles of pain and pleasure, becomes compelling. Yet, if we view the mind as an energy field, these impulses don't deserve the excessive energy we often dispense. As observers, we can meditate, discern the actual from the illusory, and then disengage.

Discernment between the actual and the illusory isn't a lofty exercise solely for the evolved; it can be a daily practice for all.

Self-restraint is the key, allowing a person to experience pain inflicted by another with **Dama**, a form of self-restraint where one chooses not to be offended, seeking neither retaliation nor revenge.

Charity or **Daana**, in the form of giving to those less fortunate, need not be restricted by a limited income. It extends beyond material offerings to include a listening ear, an encouraging lift, or a genuine compliment—a Daana of time, action, and thought.

Compassion or **Daya** involves putting oneself in another's shoes and treating others with kindness, compassion, and respect. Andal emphasizes being kind to both self and others as a habitual practice.

Andal, with her poetic prowess, intricately weaves the small village tradition of the bridal vow into the grand tapestry of spiritual exploration. She masterfully bridges the gap between the local and the universal, refraining from dismissing the village tradition as mere folklore. Instead, she elevates it to a profound spiritual practice, unveiling the hidden depths within.

While Andal possesses profound knowledge of the esoteric dharma, she doesn't overly extol formal wisdom. Her wisdom shines through as she navigates the vast terrain of spiritual understanding. Despite her deep knowledge of sacred texts, she employs a poetic and **accessible** language, inviting spiritual curiosity among her friends. Her approach is to plant the seed of divinity in the fertile soil of simplicity.

The forest of knowledge remains open for exploration. Her poetic expressions act as beacons, guiding others to embark on their spiritual journeys with a sense of wonder and curiosity.

Through her artistry, she leaves the door ajar for each seeker to delve into the profound teachings at their own pace, fostering a harmonious blend of the local and the universal in the pursuit of the Supreme.

Pillai Lokacharya and Manavala Muni, both leaders in *Visishtadvaita* philosophy, advocate the need to destroy *Ahankara* or ego to realize the sweetness of Andal's bridal mysticism. Ego, they suggest, is like a frog in a deep well, croaking about its greatness, oblivious to the immense world beyond its limited surroundings.

Respecting people of all faiths who seek the Supreme in their unique ways extends this lofty idea. The lover and the beloved concept transmute human existence with the divine's golden brilliance. The thirst to discover a higher plane is not unique to one culture, and unity stands atop the foundation of all faiths when one parts the screen's apparent diversity. Acknowledging the divine in many avatars is the cornerstone of **Sanatana Dharma** or the eternal reality.

How Inclusive Is Divine Love?

"Prajña Chakshu" involves viewing the world through knowledge, with an in-built component of humility. Knowledge intertwined with divinity perceives all creatures, big, and small, as *equal fragments of God*.

In the third verse of the Tiruppavai, the poet implores the Absolute for prosperity for creatures big and small, highlighting *our interconnectedness*.

The Supreme doesn't discriminate, and it's the devotee's responsibility to sift the grain from the chaff. In *Etrakalangal*

(Verse 21), the poet sheds light on the divine's acceptance of hostile foes turned devotees, emphasizing *forgiveness*, and *inclusivity*.

While few may be born divine, everyone is hardwired to cultivate divinity as a habit. Mistakes are part of the spiritual journey, and one can return to the path through forgiveness, persistence, patience, and discipline.

Andal's verses prompt reflection on richness beyond ego confines, urging a conscious surrender. They emphasize that ego-driven pursuits may offer a semblance of wealth but often miss the true abundance derived from a connection with the divine. The surrender becomes a conscious choice to step into the expansive realm of true richness, unburdened by the constraints of egoic attachments.

How does Andal bring the higher consciousness in the daily?

Beyond the fervor of life's orchard, there lies a profound contemplation—a silent witnessing of the divine play. The poet gazes upon the cosmic spectacle, recognizing the eternal truth that transcends transient manifestations.

Andal's genius lies in her ability to distill the esoteric into the accessible. Through the devotion of a maiden, she unravels the intricacies of the Upanishadic wisdom, making it relatable to hearts yearning for divine connection. The simple yet profound realization echoes—the seeker, entwined in life's offerings, must also be the silent observer, recognizing the unchanging amidst the changing.

The concept, often considered abstract, and metaphysical, becomes a poignant reflection in Andal's verses. It resonates in her unwavering pursuit, where the dance of the individual soul and the divine unfold in the grand playhouse of existence. The tree, laden with the fruits of karma, becomes the backdrop for Andal's exploration—a quest for oneness, where the seeker and the divine are intertwined in a sacred dance of love and surrender.

I am Siruparai, the Small Drum, echoing the heartbeat of devotion. As I walk step by step with my poet and her friends, my beats share our tale. Vedas and Upanishads may be complex, but Andal distilled their purest essence into a simple truth. She offered it to unassuming yet exalted seekers, guiding them to the infinite facets of divinity through unadulterated devotion and love from the soul's depths. Is it any surprise to discover that I too am part of this unity?

CHAPTER 16

The Gu-Ru

Who, then, is a Guru? A Guru is the one who dispels the darkness of ignorance, much like removing the film of dust from a sparkling gem. In Andal's verses, we find the essence of a true Guru – one who uncovers the divine fire within, guiding devotees to ideal ways of quenching their spiritual thirst.

An ideal teacher, in perfect attunement with the reality of the Supreme, pursues lofty goals. Such a Guru freely imparts knowledge to those open to receiving, never withholding the wisdom necessary for spiritual growth.

Andal, in every sense of the word, embodies the spirit of a Guru. Through her verses, she ignites the flame of spirituality, leaving an indelible mark on those with open minds. Yet, she doesn't linger as a Guru in the hearts she illuminates but as a devoted soul.

Is her path the sole route to the Supreme?

In the Vishnu Purana and the Skanda Purana, a profound thought echoes: *"As droplets of rain join the ocean, so will the worship of any divine deity take you to One God."*

Andal, referring to the Lord as Ranganatha, understands that divinity transcends labels and limitations. Religion and names serve as starting points, and she acknowledges the arbitrariness of these identifiers.

The routes to the Divine are diverse – through philosophies, wise Gurus, and even different religions. However, the destination remains the journey of each soul merging with the formless, nameless, and life-giving force.

Amid our mortal existence, the universal code of kindness, honesty, absence of malice, and love emerged across distant corners of the globe.

Jesus, a carpenter's son, preached love, and forgiveness, echoing teachings found in distant deserts. The diversity in understanding the Supreme, be it Allah, or Yahweh, doesn't negate the unity underlying the search for a higher force.

Rituals serve as initiatory and bonding practices, placing the uninitiated on the divine path. Gurus act as scaffolds – some need them, while others don't – but ultimately, the journey must be walked alone.

A great teacher, be it Kabir weaving spiritual poems or Meera abandoning royalty for divine love, guides with humility, and by example. The Bhagavad Gita's wisdom emphasizes that people imitate the actions of an ideal person, underscoring the importance of leading by example. In the third chapter of the Bhagavad Geeta, verse 21 refers to the actions of that kind of ideal person.

Whatever the ideal person does, people imitate. The standard that the ideal person sets, other people follow.

A true leader is not defined by high status but by guidance. Kabir, Meera, Rabia, and Joan of Arc, among others, exemplify this connection-seeking spirit despite facing criticism and opposition.

The hallmark of a genuine guru is selfless humility.

The world will and must have critics and doubters. To have spiritual knowledge is to hold the rarest gem, but to a doubter, it is a common pebble. There is a potential seeker in everyone, although the will to seek must only come from within.

Chapter 17

Love

What is Love?

Love, the highest form of spiritual connection, demands recognition, preservation, and nurturing. In Hindu philosophy, Krishna personifies love, providing a path for both the ready and the unwilling to love Him with devotion. It is universal, unselfish, accepting, and transformational—an end.

Extending beyond devotees, love is the Absolute's way of connecting with humanity. Krishna's humility as a charioteer makes Him approachable, enabling devotees to realize His greatness. Andal's teachings guide us to recognize the Divine in daily life, addressing mortality, and sin. Dispelling ignorance involves differentiating man-made constructs from the Divine and breaking free from attachments preventing connection with the Higher Self.

Is there a difference between Love and the Supreme?

Love must be recognized, preserved, nurtured, shared, and accepted. It transcends religion and rituals, existing inherently in all. Love is divinity, and divinity is love.

Krishna, in Hindu philosophy, embodies love, and union with Him represents the highest form of spiritual love. This multifaceted concept of love is intricate, requiring observation for true understanding.

Pure love manifests in various forms. The Alwars perceived the Divine as a loving consort, an approachable child, in mountains, clouds, sky, and elements. They recognized the Supreme as a nurturing mother and an awe-inspiring protector.

In the Bhagavad Gita, Krishna opens the path to love for both those ready and unwilling, emphasizing its universal, unselfish, and transformative nature. Love is not attached to results; it is an end.

Other cultures echo the importance of love. Poet Bulleshah emphasizes its priceless nature, stating, "Love is priceless, and it can never be weighed by the same scales one weighs material wealth."

Love is limitless, defying comparison.

Andal's verses beautifully convey the limitlessness of love through her unconditional devotion to the divine, particularly Lord Krishna. Her love transcends earthly boundaries, using inclusive language that embraces all of creation—flora, fauna, animate, and inanimate objects. The eradication of ego in the union with the divine showcases the boundless nature of her devotion, where individual identity conjoins not dissolves in the ocean of love.

Love is not reserved for devotees alone; the Absolute also craves it. Krishna's humility as a charioteer signifies His approachability, allowing devotees to realize His greatness. Andal refers to this in one of her verses, conveying an apology.

In the *Karavaigal Pinshendru* verse, devotees infused with love suddenly realize the astounding quality of the Absolute. They apologize if they gave Him reason to think they might have taken advantage of His humility and access.

Love is Surrender.

Ego sullies love. Why is individual surrender challenging when the Supreme surrenders in the unique reversal of master-servant? Krishna assumes the role of a lowly charioteer for Arjuna during the latter's spiritual conundrum. Just as the devotee serves the Supreme, the vice-versa is also true. This is the highest form of spiritual love. Krishna's love is never sectarian; it is universal.

Scriptures, stories, and knowledge are enjoyable, and illuminating, but without planting, nurturing, and revering seeds of love, the knowledge is futile.

Love is Selfless

Andal, as the poet, shows us one way to reach divine love without insisting on dependence or subservience to her method. Despite guiding us, she chose to become one of the devotees— an act of a selfless guide and leader.

Knowledge alone cannot make one a guru. While dispelling ignorance, a guru must go beyond preaching, being willing, like our poet, to be open to inquiry and corrections, and to step down from a lofty perch to become one with the students when necessary.

Instances exist where misled seekers fall prey to charlatans and deceptive leaders. There is an innate need to connect to something higher, but charismatic yet selfish individuals feed seekers with distortions and misrepresentations within a philosophical structure.

Love Does Not Judge.

Throughout this journey, there is a constant attempt to differentiate man-made constructs from the Divine with the idea of attachment. Attachment to matter prevents one from reaching the Higher Self, creating bondages with a compulsive, not conscious, thinking process.

What is the relationship between love, mortality, and sin?

Seeking to acquire something without consequence leads to turbulence and endless conflicts. A Law of Causality seems to govern, and the poet guides us through a conscious path to attain a divine goal.

The Supreme is not a judge; individuals are equipped to opt for intellectual thought, propelling them to make choices on how to act. The responsibility for actions and consequences lies in the hands of individuals.

In the twenty-first verse, titled "Yetra Kalangal," the girls passionately implore the Divine to embrace them in their simplicity. They hold love and kinship, and they have not harmed anyone. They question the Omniscient willingness to accept former foes who have committed sins more readily than them, unintentionally revealing a lingering sense of comparison rooted in ego. This subtle expression of ego underscores the human tendency to measure one's worthiness against others, a quality that stands in contrast to the Supreme's boundless and impartial love. Andal delicately captures the complexity of human emotions and ego in the quest for divine acceptance.

Chapter 18

Good and Evil

Good and Evil are two sides of the same coin. Cultivating the Divine Spirit is about elevating life to higher possibilities where every being, sentient, or insentient, is treated with compassion, love, and forgiveness.

Do Good and Evil exist differently in various faith systems?

A true believer in the Divine, regardless of time, place, or faith, emphasizes qualities over stories, narratives, labels, and appearances.

If we sift through these factors to isolate common strands of thought, there is a tendency to avoid vices and baser impulses while nurturing virtues and nobility of thought in almost all cultures.

For instance, kindness, valued thousands of years ago, remains the same quality today. Generosity, grace, forgiveness – virtues stand the test of time. Stories and narratives may evolve into myths and legends, but the timeless qualities endure.

Breaking down these virtues and vices, they are inherent in preserving, protecting, or destroying humankind. "virtue" aims for preservation, while "vice" contributes to annihilation.

This viewpoint extends to environmental factors. The earth may survive without creatures, but without responsible stewardship, our time may run out, much like the fate of dinosaurs.

The poet upholds virtues to cultivate the cognition of godliness: compassion, kindness, steadfastness, fortitude, peacefulness, equanimity, generosity to others, and self, non-violence in thought, speech, and action, service to others, humility, absence of covetousness, mental strength, and renunciation of certain qualities.

The concept of renunciation is not about isolating oneself in a material world; rather, it involves giving up ostentation, hypocrisy, arrogance, rage, self-conceit, ego, greed, excessive indulgences, envy, and indifference.

Liberation and bondage are not distant concepts reserved for an afterlife; they exist in the present. Consider an individual burdened by desires and possessions at the market – the baggage becomes an encumbrance, revealing the limits of their capacity. Even a simple act like bingeing on food comes with the consequence of an upset stomach.

Similarly, a person fixated on acquiring possessions in life may, at the threshold of death, realize the impermanence of material wealth. Reflecting on missed opportunities for kindness, she wishes she had spent a life giving to herself and others, making positive differences for all. This reflection underscores the profound impact of choices made in the present on one's sense of liberation or bondage.

Goals, whether short or long-term, can incorporate an understanding of the true nature of the Self. Recognizing kindness, acknowledging it with gratitude, and reciprocating, or replicating it with empathy are ways to incorporate the Divine.

Misapprehensions often cloud our perceptions. Entitlement, a misapprehension, can hinder the appreciation of a kind act. Reevaluating events without the veil of incomplete ideas and emotions allows clarity and wisdom to prevail.

Divinity surrounds us, and to unveil it, one must pierce through the temporary.

Chapter 19

Understanding Religion and Spirituality

The persistent question around me begs exploration. Why do people practice various religions worldwide? It can't be mere coincidence; there must be a purpose. Everything in existence seems to have a reason, including religion. It serves as a man-made guide to comprehend the Supreme.

However, a cautious approach is necessary before fully embracing man-made doctrines. Amid the wheat of wisdom, there is bound to be a chaff of fallacies. The true essence of any religion lies in its humanity. In its purest form, most religions share the common goal of connecting with a higher plane. Love, service, fairness, respect, and compassion for all creatures, sentient, and insentient, act as sparks that transcend religious boundaries.

Diverse paths exist for individuals to understand and connect with divinity. There isn't a singular correct way, and religion, being limited, leaves room for everyone. The Rig Veda emphasizes the Oneness of Reality, acknowledging that wise individuals may express it in multiple ways. The analogy of blind men encountering an elephant illustrates the fallacy of perceiving the Infinite through limited perspectives. Truth, inherently inexpressible, demands a deeper understanding, and respect for diverse viewpoints.

Religion initiates the spiritual quest for many, yet when it takes precedence over Supreme consciousness, it limits discovery, akin to the blind men failing to comprehend the entirety of the elephant. The seer Adi Shankara references this parable to caution against viewing the Divine with limited perspectives.

This limitation arises when religious facets are confused for the infinite whole, especially when religion supersedes devotion. Andal, the poet, echoes this sentiment. She urges seekers to shed ego, practice selfless debate, and embrace corrections—an embodiment of a selfless guide and loving devotee. Loving and surrendering to the Highest is an important aspect of her guidance.

Love and Surrender

Andal's teachings delve into the realm of love, emphasizing its selflessness, and divinity. Love, personified by Krishna in Hindu philosophy, is universal, unattached to results, and transformative. It extends beyond devotees, connecting the Absolute with humanity. Krishna's humility as a charioteer makes the Supreme approachable, a path open to both the ready and the hesitant.

Andal exemplifies the path to divine love, advocating for humility, openness to inquiry, and a willingness to step down from a pedestal to connect with students. Love, she suggests, is the key to recognizing the Divine in daily life, dispelling ignorance, and breaking free from attachments.

But is love selfish? Andal, through her poetry, exemplifies a selfless guide and devotee, emphasizing the importance of recognizing divinity in daily living by connecting to the highest frequency.

The poet's teachings on morality and sin revolve around differentiating man-made constructs from the Divine. Attachments to material matters hinder connection with the Higher Self, leading to a conscious path to attain a divine goal. Surrender to Dharma, as reflected in Andal's verses, is crucial in the journey of discovering the greater Self.

Chapter 20

The Greater Self

The truest essence in all religion lies in its humaneness. In their purest form, most religions provide similarity in wanting to connect to a higher plane, although they have different names. In the quest for the Divine, the religion's worth is only to initiate. The spark comes from love, service, fairness, respect, and compassion for sentient, and insentient creatures.

We all try to understand and connect with divinity in various ways. There is not one right way. Religion is limited, but to understand the Infinite, there is room for everyone.

A few seekers have found divinity independent of rituals. They are a rare breed. Most beings need some frame of reference.

Whether a seeker walks alone or in a group, the connection to the Supreme can only happen with devotion and complete surrender of personal ego. The ego makes the infinite choice finite by letting a sense of imperfection and sorrow pervade it. One who has annihilated ego and identified self with the Spirit, comes out of a stupor with a discriminating mind. Such a person will not allow external circumstances to cause turbulence and crush the self.

In the enchanting narrative of the Chandogya Upanishad, the tale of young Svetaketu unfolds; a journey embarked upon to acquire the profound knowledge of the Supreme, *Brahmagnana*. Returning home, his mind adorned with the wisdom of Vedas, Upanishads, and scriptures, Svetaketu exudes a subtle conceit in listing his acquired knowledge.

His father, perceptive to the essence beyond scholarly wisdom, queries if he sought the knowledge of the Supreme. Puzzled by his father's enigmatic remark, Svetaketu listens as his father imparts a profound truth: true knowledge transcends the audible, perceives the imperceptible, and comprehends the unknowable—knowledge that is grounded in the core of our being.

The father elucidates through analogies, invoking the essence within the clay to understand all clay-made objects, the grain of gold to fathom limitless golden creations, and the tiny seed within a *nygrodha* or banyan as the essence of the towering tree—a testament to the potential of a subtle essence embedded in seemingly insignificant seeds.

This profound teaching leads Svetaketu to the realization that knowledge is infinite and that the Supreme, *Parabrahman*, is omnipotent, hidden in every heart as a nameless and formless energy. Devotees access this divinity in various ways, as illustrated by the poet Andal, who identifies this energy as her lover and consort, the equal, and the peerless.

The journey of the young lasses in Andal's verses mirrors the quest for divine realization. Initially oblivious, they awaken to spirituality, sifting through the ephemeral to discern the immutable and permanent. Facing the Divine, akin to a theophany, they no longer shy away from the effulgence, breaking down lofty qualities with simple analogies.

In the culmination of their spiritual journey, the girls perceive no difference between themselves and the Divine, achieving a self-actualized state. It all commences with the innocent gaze of a young lass, seeking love as a bride to the eternal Ranganatha. The connection with the Divine, depicted as pure love between the bride and groom, becomes a timeless metaphor for devotees as spiritual brides yearning for union with the Supreme.

Amidst the discourse of not attaching oneself to anything, the understanding of the Self is illuminated. The essence lies in recognizing the infinitude within, navigating the world with wisdom, and embracing the boundless love that unites the seeker with the Divine.

Understanding the Self is not to escape from the world, but to engage with it.

Engagement with the World

In the intricate tapestry of existence, the question of how one engages with the world unfolds as a central theme. Andal, the poet, weaves together anecdotes from everyday life, presenting a choice: the path of dharma. Themes of kindness, non-violence, gratitude, empathy, and awareness of the temporary permeate her verses. Life's dualities, prosperity, and adversity are seen as temporary states, and attachment to either is deemed superfluous.

Mortals, often bound by intellectual and mental inertia in comfort, are urged to break free through engagement in activity. In the active stage, energy surges, development unfolds, and a natural inclination towards serving others may arise. Ego relinquishes its grip, transforming into dedication and, eventually, devotion. Recognizing finite objects in the material world becomes a challenge, and two methods—*Sankhya* and *Yoga*—are presented to imbue divinity into action.

Andal's verses traverse this journey, revealing both methods to be seamlessly intertwined. The Sankhya method, requiring the renunciation of agency, unveils the insignificance of individual ego. The Yoga method emphasizes unwavering action without being entangled in desires for rewards. Both paths converge toward the same goal.

Engagement in the world, according to Andal, doesn't necessitate renouncement, she acknowledges human desires, and their fulfillment, while nurturing self and others, and living harmoniously, connecting generously within a community. This communal life, depicted in her verses, fosters spiritual growth, akin to exercising the mind for equipoise. External instability loses its power over a mind honed through this practice.

Amidst the discourse of detachment, the understanding of the Self isn't an escape but an active participation in the world. Andal's verses echo the sentiment that engagement lies in recognizing the infinitude within, navigating the world with wisdom, and embracing boundless love that unites the seeker with the Divine.

In times of conflict, Andal's principles of tolerance, extreme forgiveness, generosity, and non-violence resonate with Krishna's teachings. The apparent contradiction of advocating war is clarified—fighting isn't opposed to these values but serves as a call to conquer internal and external adversaries. The battlefield, referred to as *Dharmakshetra,* or battle site to reclaim Dharma signifies the protection of dharma.

One needs to examine what truly constitutes a fight. The dialog between Krishna and Arjuna takes place after all, just before the great Kurukshetra war. It is the seeker who sees the figurative aspect. The unevolved dismiss it as a fight between kin, clan, kingdom, or a fight for a fight. It is a huge leap to hold a state of equanimity in turbulent times. The action we must take after attaining this equanimity is our duty. There's a reason this battle is referred to also as *Dharmakshetra,* conveying the idea that it's held at the battlefield to safeguard Dharma. A fight can be internal; it's a call for action to conquer jealousy, slovenliness, greed, vindictiveness, and baser qualities. A fight can be standing up to a schoolyard bully when he or she picks on a vulnerable person. Even a child has the potential to be an upstander, a bystander, or a bully. A fight can be standing up for oneself when confronted with injustice. A fight can be to dispel prejudice, ignorance, and biases that harm, or hurt an innocent.

A fight can be one to subdue arrogance, ego, and superciliousness. We straddle two sides all the time. The spiritual significance of this battle is letting the light reign over the baser impulses within us. Life has a way of turning up difficult situations. It is important to reject a defeatist mindset. With critical thought, fortitude, and sincerity, an individual can face up to solve the toughest situation.

There's always a fight between dharmic action and adharmic action, and even between action, and nonaction. A fight can be collective activism when faced with a global pandemic or a natural disaster. One must discern between the just and the unjust fight before engaging in the fight.

Sometimes, standing up for what is right may bring about the loss of friends, ridicule, and public shaming. It takes fortitude to keep the inner core from crumbling to get past the naysayers. Further, if there is no attachment to the fruits of action, one can get past without inner turbulence and fear.

Acting without a selfish desire for the betterment of both the individual and the world remains a perennial struggle, demanding enlightened, and awakened engagement. It necessitates the discernment to choose true battles and the capacity to act without attachment to the results, echoing the profound teachings of Krishna.

Andal's verses delve into the expansive concept of consciousness, moving beyond the confines of the brain's electro-chemical signals. According to her, consciousness represents the fundamental reality of existence. Drawing parallels with different states of consciousness—wakeful, dream, and thought-free sleep—Andal's verses emphasize the elevation of consciousness beyond material attachments, providing a holistic perspective on life and nurturing inner peace.

Addressing a diverse audience on their spiritual journey, Andal highlights four types of devotees, mirroring Krishna's categorization in the Bhagavad Gita. Whether distressed, seekers of knowledge, pursuers of worldly possessions, or the wise, all are expressions of the Self. Andal's verses celebrate unity in diversity, transcending ego, and divisions, recognizing each devotee's unique pace of evolution. The culmination results when consciousness is liberated from material attachments. This state enables engagement in daily life or discharging one's duties without anxiety nor fear while navigating the temporal realm with detachment.

Andal's perspective on surrender goes beyond conventional boundaries, symbolized by the dance between a maiden and Lord Krishna. This surrender is depicted as a transformative shedding of ego, leading to spiritual liberation. It transcends the physical realm, embracing an experiential dimension beyond the mundane. The indescribable nature of the Supreme is alluded to urging a transcendence of limited perceptions. The eternal union of the devotee and the divine in the quest for Ultimate Reality embodies the profound spiritual journey envisioned by Andal.

In essence, acting without selfish desires demands enlightened engagement, while the exploration of consciousness becomes a conduit for acquiring knowledge, mysterious, and internal regardless of our focus on the outer world or inner mind. Andal's verses beautifully convey the idea that the soul radiates consciousness at different levels, marking the journey of devotees as they deepen their spirituality while fulfilling their worldly duties.

Her depiction of sleep in her verses offers a unique perspective on consciousness and its stages. In the wakeful state (*Jagrut*), consciousness is outward-focused, keenly aware of the material aspects of the outer world. Andal draws parallels with the bridal vow, the unique qualities of the lasses, and the material items needed for the vow, showcasing preoccupation with the external.

Transitioning to the dreamlike state (*Svapna*), consciousness turns inward, experienced through the mind in dreams where the body may not necessarily partake. Andal invites us to consider this state, emphasizing the subjective reality of dreams that transcends scientific measurements.

Moving beyond is the thought-less or thought-free state, the deep, dreamless sleep (*Sushupti*), where consciousness separates, and roams freely. Andal suggests that stopping consciousness is not the solution; it's a symptom rather than the cause.

Raising consciousness, as Andal describes it, liberates individuals from the pleasure and pain associated with the finite and ever-changing world. It enables a holistic understanding, transcending limiting snapshots. The journey of the lasses through these stages culminates in a stage of pure consciousness, where engagement is free from anxiety or fear reaching the *Turiya* state.

- **Consciousness Beyond the Physical:** Andal's portrayal suggests that consciousness is not confined to the physical realm or the brain's electro-chemical signals. By highlighting the distinct nature of each state of sleep, she implies that there's a dimension of consciousness that transcends the material and extends into the realms of the metaphysical.
- **Spiritual Journey as a Wakeful Dream:** The journey of the lasses through these states can be seen as a metaphor for the spiritual journey. The wakeful state represents engagement with the material world, the dreamlike state signifies internal exploration and reflection, and the deep, dreamless sleep reflects a state of heightened consciousness and transcendence.

- **Unity in Consciousness:** Andal's focus on the Oneness of Self, regardless of the varied states of consciousness, ties into the idea that the core of our being remains unchanged. This unchanging core, akin to the seer within, experiences the different states of consciousness but remains steadfast and unadulterated.
- **Surrender and Transcendence:** The surrender that Andal advocates, especially in the *Turiya* state, aligns with the idea of transcending the limitations of ordinary consciousness. It's a surrender of the ego and individual identity, akin to the shedding of dreams and thoughts in the deep, dreamless sleep state.

In essence, Andal's exploration of sleep states becomes a metaphorical journey through consciousness, connecting the physical, mental, and spiritual aspects of human existence. It underscores the profound nature of consciousness and its connection to the divine, weaving a tapestry that goes beyond the ordinary boundaries of perception.

The common thread among all beings is the Self, the impartial conscious principle that exists in everyone. Andal connects this concept with the law of karma, emphasizing that the joy, and sorrow one experiences are proportional to what is contributed to the universe. Love and devotion, dispensed with mindful awareness of the Self, result in reciprocity.

The poet delves into the profound idea of the Oneness of Self. The unchanging seer within everyone takes in all components of the mind, guiding like an inner voice. Despite starting at different points in their level of Divine consciousness, the girls end up in the fourth category due to their spiritual engagement. The focus is both inward and outward simultaneously, a true engagement in life's duties without disturbance to the mind. Absolute peace reigns, and the pull of earthly games fades at this elevated plane, where the world's temporality is seen with complete detachment.

Andal, through her verses, acknowledges the diversity in living forms, ranging from Gopika to seers, bees, birds, cows, and the entire fauna, and flora. Yet, this diversity pales in comparison to the countless avatars the Lord assumes to protect devotees. From Keshava to Madhusudana, Govinda to Krishna, and Narayana, the limitless aspect of the Divine is reflected. In this diversity lies the profound Oneness.

The second verse, *Ongiulagalanda*, encapsulates a prayer for prosperity for all creatures and phenomena, symbolizing a plea for unshakable prosperity for the universe. It seeks an unchanging, permanent union with the Supreme, highlighting the divine bond in collective prosperity.

Abundance is a recurring theme in Andal's poems from start to finish. The thirty verses culminate on the harvest festival day of Pongal, meaning overflow. First, the idea of plentiful supply highlights a sense of surge. The underlying premise is that the universe is abundant and expansive when lived with noble principles.

Humans tend to hold on to something or want more of the same thing when they possess a scarcity mindset. This fear can block access to the ever-expanding energy. Instead, one can repose unwavering conviction in divinity, beauty, and the power of love to share. Leaning into the spiritual power, one can create, share, and receive an authentic, and benevolent life. In the middle poems *elle elankiliye* and *kutuvillakeriya*, there's a sense of selfishly holding on to the divine. This sentiment comes from a place of paucity, from a constricted space. The universe is limitless, and it is forever expanding.

For far too long, we have succumbed to the conversation of scarcity. It could be complaining about what we do not possess instead of choosing to appreciate what we have. However, the universe is expansive, and swapping the fear of scarcity with the idea of abundance is accomplished when tuning into the spiritual potential. The universe sustains us all, and prosperity can be achieved when we imagine the universe as energy and not just matter.

The idea of spaciousness amplifies the value of self-worth over net worth.

The Goddess Lakshmi as Kamalatmika symbolizes spaciousness and beauty. Seated on a lotus, the beauteous one rises high and pure while rooted in material muck. She embodies fame, fortune, fertility, and material, and spiritual riches. With her blessings, the land yields crops, businesses turn over profits, and good luck pervades the microcosm. She is the compassionate giver and ensures prosperity for all her devotees. She is the antithesis of famine, barrenness, and constriction. Moving from the microcosm to the macrocosmic level through her poems, the cowherd girls record their spiritual sojourn of spaciousness.

As a compassionate giver, Lakshmi rules the outer material at the concrete level. Material abundance, when used to create space for others, brings forth joy. At the highest level, she is the necessary partner to the Almighty, known as Sriman Narayana, unfolding divinity into realms of action and creation.

The girls expanded possibilities by tuning into their spiritual frequencies, working together, and opening their eyes to nurture the macrocosm for all creatures hard at work.

Verse 21, *Yetra Kalangai* is a plea to the Supreme to recognize their selfless devotion flowing like unlimited milk from the most generous cows. Their open mindset for spiritual acceptance manifests through the outflowing energy of uncontainable divine love. While sacred scriptures help understand the complexity of the Almighty, pure love in service to all creatures augments the *outflow* idea of energy. After all, isn't there creator divinity in all creations?

How then does one increase the outflow energy?

First, one must blur the lines between the material and spiritual world by letting go of the selfish hold on things. The universe expands to provide more for the individual by creating space for others bringing forth a joyful state of being or reciprocal gifts.

Andal's verses weave a tapestry where inanimate objects, seasons, and the entire universe converge into an underlying unity in the Absolute. This realization fosters inclusion, unity, strength, and empowerment of the individual within the collective. There is no room for ego, divisions, or arbitrary classifications.

The poet acknowledges the existence of the Supreme beyond the dualities of earthbound life, urging us to transcend our limited perceptions. One can draw parallels with the unseen colors perceived by a praying mantis or the heightened auditory senses of a dog, emphasizing that the divine is present in plain sight if one chooses to "see."

The indescribable nature of the Supreme is a recurring theme, with Andal suggesting that the facets of this divine energy can only be hinted at. In the quest for self-discovery, the truth emerges as a simple proclamation, *"Tat Tvam Asi"* or "Absolute You are." Andal's take on surrender, as portrayed in her heartfelt verses, serves as an inspiration for those navigating the path of devotional surrender in the Bhakti tradition. The imagery of a gentle separation, with the understanding that the devotee and the divine are eternally united in the quest for the Ultimate Reality, encapsulates the essence of Andal's profound spiritual journey.

In the rhythmic resonance of my beats, I am not merely a drum; I am a vessel of spiritual transformation. As the echoes subside, I bear witness to the devotee's profound metamorphosis—a testament to the profound impact of Andal's teachings.

Through the tapestry of unity, love, and self-realization woven by Andal, the devotee journeys to the highest state of consciousness. In this state of blissful union, the individual, and Self merge seamlessly. My beats fade into silence, echoing the call to awaken consciousness and surrender to the divine.

As the drum, I stand as a silent witness to the devotee's evolution—a rhythmic ode to the transformative power of devotion and the eternal dance of the soul.

With a gentle grace of one hand, she delicately pulls me out from under the crook of the other, placing me down. Though physically apart, the unspoken understanding lingers—we are in this together, forever entwined in the ceaseless quest for the Ultimate Reality.

Chapter 21

Author's Reflection

Until this point, the author used the drum as a narrating device. Seeking forgiveness for any transgressions, she will, in the third person, present a modest exercise to infuse Andal's glorious spirit to add depth to daily life. Andal's impassioned verses form a delicate garland draped over her beloved's shoulders, akin to a devout hug.

Andal aspired to attain *Prapatti*, total surrender to the Divine, through her poetry. She serves as a spiritual cartographer, beginning with the individual self and infusing humanity, compassion, love, faith, and the surrender of ego in touching divinity.

The depth with which one chooses to explore the spiritual journey in all its layers, textures, and nuances, is a personal one at a self-driven pace. The author believes that life is an open gym for spirituality. Her exercise offering, while not acrobatic, takes the form of an acrostic P*O*E*M exercise, honoring the beautiful poetry Andal once created. More than ten centuries later, they continue to hold and grow in relevance. The author hopes the reader finds beauty in the mundane by infusing the poet's everlasting spirit through verse. Acrostic Gym of Spirituality P*O*E*M*

P (Poetry): In the verses of Andal, the beauty lies not just in the divine themes but in the literary aspects and figures of speech she employs. The concrete beginnings of her poems, often rooted in daily living, showcase innocence, and relatability. As we savor the literary nuances, we acknowledge the devotee's earnest entreaties for material needs, understanding that the journey from the little world to the larger universe is a pathway leading towards the divine.

O (Observation): Observation of Andal's poems involves exploring diverse meanings, asking questions, and navigating from the microcosm to the macrocosm. Her narratives and metanarratives provide a lens through which we learn about others, delve into infinite layers within the soul, and witness the Creator's majesty—from the diminutive *Vamana* to the mind-defying *Vishwaroopam*.

E (Engagement): The relevance of Andal's words to modern life becomes apparent as we engage with her wisdom. The author, through the P.O.E.M. exercise, seeks to apply appreciation, and observation to the layers of the self. Can we, in our contemporary existence, draw upon the poet's viewpoint to navigate life's complexities and seek higher truths?

M (Movement): Movement, in the context of Andal's verses, is the translation of energy into positive action. The hope is that the P.O.E.M. exercise propels readers into positive action. By incorporating the wisdom from Andal's poetry into our daily lives, we become instruments of positive change. This movement involves not only personal transformation but also contributes to the well-being of those around us.

Andal's verses, through the P.O.E.M. framework, guide us not just to explore the realms of divinity but also inspire us to manifest these reflections into tangible actions. The wisdom distilled from her poetry becomes a catalyst for positive change, fostering a harmonious existence, and an interconnected world enriched by the timeless truths she unfolds.

As we engage in acts of kindness, compassion, and love, we become conduits of the divine bliss that Andal alludes to in her verses. Helping others and ourselves through positive actions is a manifestation of our spiritual journey—a journey inspired by Andal's poetic wisdom.

By assessing the tangible results of our positive actions, we gain insight into the transformative power of kindness and selflessness. The ripple effect of our deeds extends beyond the immediate moment, contributing to a collective wave of positivity in the world.

In recognizing the divine bliss that emanates from these activities, we come full circle to Andal's teachings. The joy derived from selfless acts becomes a testament to the profound connection between our actions and the divine presence. Andal's poetry, like a guiding light, encourages us to not only explore but also embody the spiritual principles she beautifully articulates, fostering a world enriched by love, compassion, and divine bliss.

DAY 1

Margazhi Thingal

The Beginning

In this first verse, Andal unfolds the awe-inspiring form of Narayana, recognizing that the young maidens may not grasp the full majesty at this stage of their spiritual journey. To bridge the understanding, she adheres to tradition, promising the divine gift of *Parai*, which the maidens interpret as a drum from Narayana. The anticipation is palpable, as they enthusiastically plan to engage in joyful activities like playing, singing, or dancing with the promised gift.

P*O*E*M Exercise

DAY 1

Margazhi Thingal

The Month of Margazhi

Behold the full moon in the season of Margazhi!

Dear bejeweled girls, thriving in prosperous Brindavan! Join along if you desire. Let us bathe with thoughts of Narayana, who is the son of Nandagopa. This lion cub of Yashoda holds the sharp foe-defeating spear while his eyes are filled with love. Let us reflect on his dark form, brilliant red eyes and face like the moon. Only Narayana can bestow the Parai or drum.

Join us, and let the people of the world celebrate this union.

P (Poetry):

The initial step in a spiritual journey is recognizing the realm beyond the oblivious self. Referring to the Supreme as Narayana, Andal vividly describes His physical attributes and intense presence, setting the stage for a divine revelation. The Supreme is portrayed with cosmic symbolism, and the richness of the description reflects the grandeur that awaits the maidens. While the young seekers may not fully comprehend the magnitude of Narayana's form, Andal's verses sow the seeds of curiosity, promising a deeper revelation through the sacred *Parai*. Without expanding on the nuanced word *Parai*, she leaves it to the young maidens who interpret it as the gift of the drum.

This strategic approach aligns with Andal's wisdom, recognizing the importance of meeting the devotees at their current level of understanding and gradually guiding them toward profound spiritual insights. The promise of the divine drum becomes a tangible symbol, a catalyst for the maidens' spiritual journey, as they eagerly await the transformative experiences that lie ahead. Andal's poetic narrative unfolds like a sacred tapestry, weaving the anticipation of divine revelation into the very fabric of the seekers' lives.

O (Observation): In observing the first verse, Andal displays a profound understanding of spiritual guidance. Rather than revealing the full power and majesty of the Supreme, she delicately chooses to withhold certain aspects. This intentional restraint is a masterstroke in spiritual mentoring, reflecting Andal's wisdom as a compassionate spirit guide.

The decision not to overwhelm the young maidens with the full force of the divine showcases Andal's deep empathy and insight into the human psyche. The complete unveiling of the Supreme's breathtaking form might be too much for the girls to comprehend at their current stage of spiritual exploration. It could potentially demotivate them, causing them to retreat to the comfort of the familiar material realm.

Andal, acting as a spiritual mentor, recognizes the importance of meeting the seekers where they are and providing guidance that aligns with their current capacity for understanding. By gradually unfolding the mysteries of the divine and using symbols like the *Parai* drum to the Nonesuch *Parai*, she ensures that the young maidens remain curious, engaged, and motivated on their spiritual journey.

This thoughtful approach not only reveals Andal's role as a compassionate guide but also emphasizes the delicate balance required in spiritual mentorship. It's a testament to her profound understanding of human nature and the nuanced path of spiritual exploration. Andal's wisdom shines through, guiding the seekers with just the right amount of divine revelation to keep their hearts open and their spirits eager for more.

E (Engagement): Extending the thought to the present context, the poem becomes a beacon amid the noise of external validations and material pursuits. Andal's call to focus on ethical living and virtuous thoughts echoes as a timeless reminder to seek substance over superficiality. The concept of Dharma becomes a guiding principle in navigating the complexities of modern life.

M (Movement):

Drawing on the poet's spirit map to chart a course, she incorporates Andal's teachings into daily life by consciously choosing to prioritize the divine in daily, actions over external validations. As the author chooses to write this book, she, at times, feels overwhelmed. However, she chooses to engage in little acts of kindness, fostering empathy, and understanding towards herself to interpret greatness. Breaking the mountain-like task into individual steps, this movement towards aligning with the principles and wisdom of Dharma is a step toward genuine spiritual growth, resonating with Andal's timeless wisdom. The author reminds herself constantly that this book is for the reader. Incorporating this exercise while dealing with the daily grind helps the author build a better version of herself.

DAY 2

Vayathu Vaizhveergal

Insights and Reflections

"Oh, young maidens, let us join forces to follow these steps for conducting our vow. First, we are to obtain the Supreme. Then, when we find Him, we will hold steadfast to his feet. He's far away, in deep slumber, ignorant about our yearning, while resting on the plump coils of the infinity Adisesha.

Let's not indulge in milk, ghee, and delicacies that keep us from reaching him. Ringing the eyes with kohl or enhancing physical beauty with fragrant flowers on self is useless. He's impervious to superficiality. Our goal is to reach the Divine. So, we must think good thoughts, do charitable deeds, and not use hurtful words. We must keep in the path of Dharma, for this is the way of our vow."

P*O*E*M Exercise

Andal's guidance to the young maidens in *"Vayathu Vaizhveergal"* serves as a beacon, illuminating the path to the divine through simplicity and adherence to Dharma. Let's explore the essence of the in the context of this profound guidance:

P (Poetry): Andal's verses convey the notion that mirroring divine qualities is the key to accessing elevated spirits. The simplicity of life, free from artifices, and superficial embellishments, becomes a sacred canvas to reflect the divine attributes of kindness, love, fairness, and empathy. Poetry, in this context, transcends literary expression and becomes a way of living—a poetic dance with the divine.

O (Observation): The call for mindful observation is evident in Andal's guidance. Actions ranging from inaction to superficial engagements are scrutinized through the lens of Dharma. The seekers are urged to cultivate a habit of adopting the Dharmic way of life, fostering a deeper understanding of the significance of their actions on the spiritual journey.

E (Engagement): In the contemporary context, specifically in the realm of social media, there is a tendency to view someone's seemingly perfect life. It's natural for envy, fear, or comparison to arise.

M (Movement): The essence of movement lies in translating energy into positive action. Andal's guidance prompts introspection and a commitment to betterment. If the individual consciously chooses to transform these base feelings into joy for the person, there is a mindful movement towards transformation. This intentional shift prevents them from making judgmental comments and aligns with the principles of Dharma. It's a proactive movement towards positivity, contributing not only to their well-being but also to fostering a more positive online environment.

Dharmic principles serve as precision tools, akin to a surgical knife, enabling individuals to weed out negative emotions such as envy, fears, and comparisons. Choosing kindness over judgment becomes a conscious decision—one that aligns with the principles of Dharma and propels individuals toward a higher spiritual plane. We often forget the choice we make.

What will the author choose to do today?

Today, she encounters a situation where an employee falls short on a task, and her initial reaction is to judge and criticize. Remembering Andal's guidance, she chooses kindness over judgment. Instead of reprimanding, she extends understanding and support. She considers the potential challenges the employee might be facing, acknowledges the complexities of the task, and recognizes that everyone encounters obstacles from time to time.

Despite a short delay, the resulting work exhibits higher efficiency. By choosing understanding and support over immediate judgment, a collaborative, and positive environment is fostered, contributing to enhanced productivity, and overall well-being.

In this way, the movement from judgment to the lack of it becomes a small yet impactful step on the journey of embodying divine qualities in daily interactions.

DAY 3

Ongiulaganda

Cosmic Abundance

"The Omnipotent once appeared as Vamana, a tiny lad, and he took on an infinite loftiness to show his true self. He measured the three worlds with this form. We, damsels, take His name to laud His limitless stature. Immersed in the Highest One, let us bathe, and chant the greatness.

We pray for the universe to exist without evil. We request the abundance manifesting in warm showers occurring thrice a month. Paddy's lush, tall growth in reciprocation will give out high-quality grain. This fertile growth creates a playground for fish to jump in and out, and the beautiful blooms of flowers cushion shining bees cocooned in peaceful slumber. Overflowing pails of milk from willing cows are proof of abundance. Let this prosperity and lush vegetation forever benefit all creatures in the universe."

P*O*E*M Exercise

P (Poetry): There is room for everyone in this interdependent web. In Andal's verses, the Omnipotent's manifestation as Vamana, a tiny lad, symbolizes the infinite loftiness of the divine. The poet invites damsels to laud His limitless stature through a clean mind, body, and spirit. The interconnectedness of all beings is a central theme, emphasizing the role of each unit in the grand web of existence. The idea there is abundance for all dispels the scarcity mindset.

O (Observation): Stepping into the garden, the diversity of flora, and fauna reflects the Master Artist's boundless creativity. Each leaf, with its unique colors, textures, and shapes, defies categorization under a single label. The bees, though small, contribute significantly to pollination, highlighting the intricate interdependence of nature. This observation prompts a realization of the purpose inherent in both the grand and the minute.

E (Engagement): Continuing to respect the earth's outstanding quality, the commitment extends to conscious consumer choices. One example is when people opt for products with less packaging and embrace reuse and recycling, these practices become daily habits. The conscious acknowledgment of being part of the interconnected web fosters a sense of responsibility when people act as stewards of the earth.

M (Movement):

Today, the author immersed herself in the act of creation by crafting a book from discarded materials, a humble sanctuary for her daily musings and reminders. As raindrops fell, her family decided on a mindful exercise. They ventured outside, refusing to discard vegetable peels in the trash. Despite the inconvenience of a trek to the compost bin, they embraced the opportunity to connect with the earth. Reflecting on their ability to purchase fresh vegetables, engage their senses in their preparation, and savor a nutritious meal, the family felt a profound sense of gratitude. Each peel added to the compost pile became a gift to the billions of microorganisms, contributing to the flourishing richness of the soil beneath the feet.

In these simple yet intentional actions, in this movement toward mindful stewardship of the abundant earth, the author noticed a sense of joyful privilege.

DAY 4

Azhimazhai

Recognizing the Divine Signature

"O dear Lord, we need an outpouring of rain; please do not withhold even a bit.

Your proportions are awe-inspiring. You have a majestic, dark hue, much like the rain-engorged dark sky. The glittering chakra or wheel in Padmanabha's one hand you manifest to us as lightning. Thunder is your Valampuri conch. Your divine bow Saranga shoots out arrow-like raindrops. We implore you to dispatch these without delay. The rain will help our world thrive while we frolic in these waters of the season."

P*O*E*M Exercise

P (Poetry): The poet employs metaphorical analogies to show the majesty and grandeur of the Supreme. Appreciate the divine signature in nature by observing the intricate details of your surroundings. Consider the marvel of even the smallest creatures and elements, recognizing the interconnectedness of all living beings. Marvel the majesty of the cycles and elements of nature. The poet hopes to draw the damsels from their microcosm to the macrocosm.

O (Observation): Practice mindfulness in your daily life. Notice the beauty in small things, such as the beautiful shapes and coloration in the petals of flowers, and acknowledge the diversity, and uniqueness in the natural world. Understand that every being, no matter how small, contributes to the grandeur of existence.

E (Engagement): Express gratitude for the blessings in your life and radiate positive vibes. Engage in activities that contribute positively to the environment and community. Consider participating in local initiatives, like community gardens, or environmental projects, to collectively work towards the well-being of the macrocosm.

M (Movement):

In a modern context, individuals can engage with the poem "Azhimazhai" by participating in local environmental initiatives or community gardens. Sharing plant cuttings with neighbors or joining a gardening club reflects the poet's emphasis on contributing positively to the interconnected web of life. This is just one example.

Moreover, the principles embedded in the poem can extend to larger scales, including corporate responsibility, and global initiatives. Here are some examples:

Corporate Responsibility:

Waste Reduction: Big companies can adopt sustainable practices to minimize waste generation. This involves reevaluating production processes, optimizing resource use, and implementing efficient recycling programs.

Environmental Impact Assessments: Before engaging in activities like quarrying or mining, companies can conduct thorough environmental impact assessments. This ensures that their operations do not cause irreversible harm to ecosystems.

Sustainable Mining Practices:

Reforestation Initiatives: Companies involved in mining can contribute to reforestation efforts. Planting trees helps restore ecosystems, prevent soil erosion, and mitigate the environmental impact of mining activities.

Community Engagement: Engaging with local communities is essential. Companies should involve community members in decision-making processes, address concerns, and share the benefits of their operations.

Conflict-Free Practices:

Ethical Sourcing: Companies can commit to ethical sourcing practices, ensuring that their activities do not contribute to conflicts or human rights abuses. This is particularly relevant in industries like mining and resource extraction.

Promoting Peace: Large corporations can actively support peace initiatives and contribute to conflict resolution efforts in regions affected by wars or political instability.

Global Environmental Stewardship:

Collaboration and Advocacy: Big companies can collaborate with each other and with environmental organizations to advocate for sustainable practices on a global scale. This includes promoting policies that prioritize environmental conservation and responsible resource management.

Technology and Innovation:

Green Technologies: Investing in and adopting green technologies can significantly reduce the environmental impact of industrial processes. This includes energy-efficient practices, renewable energy sources, and innovations that minimize ecological footprints.

Transparency and Accountability:

Reporting Standards: Companies can adhere to transparent reporting standards regarding their environmental impact. This fosters accountability and allows stakeholders, including consumers, and investors, to make informed decisions based on a company's sustainability practices.

By incorporating these principles into various aspects of life and business, individuals, and corporations can contribute to the well-being of the planet and promote a sustainable and harmonious existence.

DAY 5

Mayanai Mannu

The Enchanter

Here, the avatar is Lord Krishna of Mathura, the wondrous magician, and illusionist who alters the course of fate for the greater good.

He's ever-present. Take Krishna's name to rid yourself of doubts, fears, and flaws.

You may find him playing on the bank of the exalted Yamuna River at a given moment. He claims to be of cowherd lineage. A divine lamp, he brightened his mother's womb. The wondrous one is as approachable as a mischievous little boy whom Yashoda once bound up by a mere rope to keep him from running off.

Go forth with a purity of mind, body, and spirit, offer Him flowers, prostrate, and sing his praises while meditating upon him in heart and mind.

Just as a small cotton piece burns away in a raging inferno with ease, our flaws and misdeeds of the past perish by taking His name."

P*O*E*M Exercise

P (Poetry): In this poem, the poet employs the artistry of language to paint a vivid portrayal of Lord Krishna as the wondrous magician and eternal presence. The poetic imagery surrounding Krishna's activities on the banks of the Yamuna River, his divine lineage, and the mischievous escapades with mother Yashoda conveys a sense of divine accessibility. The use of metaphor, such as comparing flaws, and misdeeds to a small cotton piece burning away in an inferno, adds a poetic depth that invites contemplation.

O (Observation): On observing the poet's depiction of Krishna's accessibility, we can notice the verses encourage a profound understanding that divinity is not exclusive to a select few but is open to all, especially those who approach with purity and humility. The observation extends to recognizing the universality of making mistakes and the assurance that past misdeeds can be overcome through seeking the pure energy represented by Krishna.

E (Engagement): Engaging with the poem involves embracing the concept that spirituality is not confined to an exclusive club but is accessible to all individuals who choose to receive it. The engagement aspect emphasizes the resilience to keep trying despite failures and the commitment to fixate on higher consciousness in mind, body, and spirit. The poem's message encourages an active engagement with the divine, symbolized by offering flowers, prostrating, singing praises, and meditating on Krishna.

M (Movement): The movement inspired by the poem involves cultivating a positive spirit and staying on the path of kindness and compassion. Acknowledging the inevitability of slipping and embracing the constant exercise of shedding negativity, the individual moves forward with a sense of sufficiency. The recognition of the childlike aspect of the spirit becomes a powerful motivator to navigate stumbling blocks, knowing that the devices to reach a higher state are readily available.

Even the small act of self-care such as missing the visit to the gym can be infused with the dharma principle of recognizing stumbling blocks and forgiving self while getting back on track.

In essence, this poetry exercise encompasses the artistic expression, metaphorical richness, and imaginative language employed by the poet to convey profound spiritual insights and the accessibility of divinity to all seekers. One need not be plagued with doubt, low self-worth, or fears, as access to the Supreme is not an exclusive club membership.

DAY 6

Pullum Silambinakan

Destroying Obstacles

The poet presents a compelling case to wake up with this verse:

"Look, young maiden, the awakened birds, herald the dawn. Can you not hear them tweet? They're calling out at the temple of our Lord. They call out to the king of all birds, Garuda, who's none other than Lord Vishnu's aerial vehicle. Can you not hear the resounding call of the sacred white, bright conch blown at the Lord's temple? Open your eyes, young lass! The Leelas (magical games) of Krishna started early. Even as a little baby, he overcame and destroyed obstacles like the evil Putana, who, under Kamsa's orders, offered him poisoned milk from her teats. He sucked out the poison along with her life. He rests peacefully on the comfortable coils of Adisesha, the snake. Yet He alone is the cause of the universe. This is how the sages and Yogis, adept in meditation, always keep him in mind. They chant the mighty name several times, Hari, Hari, Hari! Reaching a thunderous crescendo, that primordial sound cannot be ignored. Let it enter your inner soul. Gently rouse, let's chant His name together. Let that sound refresh our inner selves while we finish the vow."

P*O*E*M Exercise

P (Poetry):

Using mythological demons, the poet weaves the idea of aspiring for higher consciousness. Awakening is about shedding pettiness, toxic thoughts, lethargy, and baser instincts that impede our ascent. She advocates fixating on the inner soul and connecting to divinity through meditation.

O (Observation):

Observation becomes the inaugural step—a recognition that mere physical wakefulness doesn't automatically translate into spiritual awareness. The poet, through the allegory of mythological demons, unfolds a profound narrative of spiritual awakening. This awakening is depicted as a process of shedding impediments such as procrastination and avoidance that obstruct our ascent to higher consciousness. It involves igniting the inner light, transcending pettiness, dispelling toxic thoughts, and overcoming the lethargy that binds us to mundane existence.

E (Engagement):

Inspired by the poem, the narrator adopts the sacred mantra of *Ha* and *Ri* as a deliberate practice of thought cleansing. This ritual extends beyond personal emotions, encompassing a compassionate outlook toward oneself and others. The expulsion of negative thoughts and mindless drama creates a fertile ground for the flow of constructive ideas, coupled with an openness to the surrounding grace. The harnessed powerful energy is strategically preserved to navigate challenges with a lucid and unhindered mind. Stepping into personal power becomes a transformative journey, necessitating the shedding of fear, paving the way for a purposeful life, and fostering a profound connection with the higher spirit.

M (Movement):

The book's author draws upon a personal experience, such as climbing Mount Kilimanjaro, to vividly illustrate the transformative influence of mindset. Rather than yielding to negative and limiting thoughts, the climber directs focus towards the essence of the experience, extracting invaluable life lessons. In this metaphorical journey towards spiritual summits, the climber encounters a continuous process of sliding back and forth—a perpetual and evolving expedition that surpasses mere physical peaks, delving into the enchanting realms of spiritual elevation. The inclusion of the majesty of the varied landscapes, the unsung heroes, the porters, cooks, and guides, who wear the challenges of the climb with a smile, adds a layer of gratitude and reciprocity to the narrative. Just as they express a positive attitude, the climber reciprocates their kindness, extending it to her own hesitant self. The journey becomes a dynamic exchange, fostering a collective ascent towards a higher bliss.

DAY 7

Keesukisengendru

Activate!

"Oh, sleepy girl! Do you not hear the deafening chatter of the birds? They actively converse back and forth while you are gripped in a demon-like sleep. Can you not smell the fragrant locks of the flower-bedecked girls? Their coin-like auspicious jewelry jingles as they vigorously pull at the curd churn with both hands. Oh, girl with the in-built divinity of Narayana, are you in a trance to the activity around you? The dairymaids sing in their sweetest voices about Narayana as Keshava, the slayer of Keshi, the demon. Come open the door with a pleasant and sparkling countenance. How can you, a leader of girls, linger in bed?"

P*O*E*M Exercise

P (Poetry):

Poetry unfolds as the poet gently stirs awareness, emphasizing the rhythmic balance between day and night, activity, and rest. Sleep, when viewed as restorative after engagement, takes on a transformative quality. The soul's purpose, housed within the body, is instrumental in attaining wisdom and reflecting the divine in everyday life. The body, equipped with senses, becomes a vessel to access the frequency of the highest spirit and radiate it to all of creation. The poet urges an awakening from spiritual slumber, recognizing the divine within oneself and others, and fulfilling duties in alignment with dharma principles.

O (Observation): The girl in the poem sleeps amidst the lively chatter of birds and the harmonious churning of butter by dairymaids. Yet, the poet warns against lingering in rest, as it may lead to missed opportunities to honor and care for oneself and others, tap into creative wisdom, fulfill duties, and infuse daily life with divinity.

E (Engagement): The garden nearby serves as a profound classroom, where the morning symphony of birds, the vibrant display of flowers, and the industrious work of bees highlight the interconnectedness and significance of all life. Gratitude emerges for being intricately woven into the cosmic web of existence, recognizing the intrinsic value of every living being. The garden becomes a canvas for awakening a higher power within each entity, transforming the daily grind to serve up spiritual abundance.

M (Movement): The author reflects on personal experiences, using the metaphor of falling into the "internet rabbit hole" as a real-life example. In this context, the "internet rabbit hole" refers to the phenomenon of getting engrossed in various online activities, such as reading news, checking pop-up notifications, playing an online game, responding to communication, and other online distractions, which may lead to a loss of focus and a sense of being disconnected from the present moment of writing this book.

The narrator likens this experience to indulging in a small treat, like a cookie, which can be enjoyable in moderation. However, when one indulges in online distractions without restraint, it becomes comparable to binge-eating cookies, leading to negative consequences. The repercussions may include feelings of worry, judgment, and FOMO (Fear of Missing Out), ultimately affecting the well-being, and nourishment of the spirit.

By sharing this example, she emphasizes the importance of self-awareness to extricate oneself from the trance of distractions and instead harness the potential of the five senses to tap into the sixth sense—the power of intuition and deeper understanding. This real-life illustration serves as a relatable and contemporary context within the broader themes of the poem.

DAY 8

Keezh Vaanam

Spirit Ally

"O girl, the eastern sky is now bright, and the cows, and buffaloes have briefly gone out to pasture. The girls are all ready and waiting

to leave, but a few of us have held them back because we wish to awaken you with happiness.

Arise, O girl! Let us together sing with enthusiasm for the boon we seek. Let's praise him for the brave victory over the horse-like ogre. He rid the world of the ogre's evil ways by pulling apart the equine mouth. Let us praise him for vanquishing the bad wrestlers sent to kill the innocent.

Narayana is Prime. We will prostrate in front of him. He will let us know he's listening to our concerns with compassionate 'Ahs and Ohs.' Let us seek the supreme grace from the God of gods to understand the spiritual self."

P*O*E*M Exercise

P (Poetry):

The poet conveys a sense that the Universe listens to sincere intentions, emphasizing the presence of a spiritual ally during challenges. She urges individuals to awaken their inner spirit, emphasizing that sleep does not make problems disappear. By aligning with the divine and embodying a heroic spirit within, one taps into an infinite source of strength and resilience. The inner spirit becomes a guiding force during challenges, making any obstacle surmountable. Praising the spirit's heroic deeds, the poet attempts to rouse the sleeping girl. The bright day awaits like all the eager girls. We are infinitely capable, and when the universe listens, one must pay heed to it.

O (Observation):

Awakening the Inner Spirit: In the poet's verses, the act of awakening is not just a physical stirring from sleep, but a spiritual, and mental arousal. The poet urges individuals to recognize that merely avoiding or ignoring problems, akin to remaining in a state of sleep, does not make them disappear. Instead, the invitation is to confront challenges with a heightened awareness—an awakening of the inner spirit.

Alignment with the Divine: The emphasis on aligning with the divine suggests a connection with a higher power or universal energy. This alignment is portrayed as a deliberate choice to seek guidance, support, and inspiration from a source beyond the immediate self. It's an acknowledgment that there is a profound force that can provide clarity and strength when faced with life's trials.

Embodying a Heroic Spirit: To embody a heroic spirit means adopting the qualities of courage, resilience, and determination. The poet encourages individuals to tap into their inner hero—the part of themselves capable of facing challenges head-on. This heroic spirit is not external but an intrinsic aspect of one's being, waiting to be recognized, and embraced.

Infinite Source of Strength: The notion of tapping into an infinite source of strength implies that the wellspring of resilience and fortitude resides within each person. It's a recognition that, when connected to the inner spirit and the divine, individuals can draw upon a boundless reserve of energy that goes beyond mere physical or mental capacities.

Guiding Force During Challenges: The awakened inner spirit, aligned with the divine, serves as a guiding force during challenges. It becomes a compass, providing direction, and clarity in navigating through difficulties. With this guiding force, no obstacle is considered insurmountable, as the individual draws upon the wisdom and strength flowing from the awakened spirit.

In essence, the poet's message is a powerful call to recognize the inner strength that lies dormant within everyone. It's an encouragement to awaken this spirit, align with the divine, and embrace a heroic mindset that transforms challenges into opportunities for growth, abundance, and triumph.

E (Engagement):

The poet's message prompts an exploration of one's potential and the unfolding of inner capabilities. It encourages a proactive approach to life, urging individuals to take intentional steps toward self-discovery and growth.

M (Movement):

Exploration and Experimentation: Movement in this context involves actively exploring and experimenting with one's capabilities. Just as the poet suggests awakening the inner spirit, individuals can engage in activities or endeavors that challenge and stretch their current limits. Trying new things, whether in personal, or professional domains, becomes a form of movement toward self-awareness.

Courageous Inquiry: Movement is also found in the courage to inquire within. If one does not ask or try, how will they discover the depths of their inner ally or hero? This involves introspective practices, such as journaling, meditation, or seeking guidance, creative hobbies, and business endeavors to uncover hidden strengths and aspects of oneself that may remain dormant without intentional inquiry.

Learning from Challenges: Movement encompasses the willingness to confront challenges head-on. Rather than shying away from difficulties, individuals can view them as opportunities for growth. Each challenge becomes a steppingstone in the movement toward realizing one's inner resilience and strength.

Acting: Movement is inherently tied to action. It involves implementing plans, pursuing goals, and taking tangible steps toward personal development. Whether in the context of writing a book or any other endeavor, the act of doing, trying, and persisting is a vital aspect of the movement toward self-discovery.

Iterative Progress: Movement is not always linear; it involves iterative progress. Individuals can embrace a mindset that acknowledges the importance of learning from experiences, adjusting strategies, and persisting in the face of setbacks. This iterative approach keeps the journey dynamic and forward-moving.

In essence, the movement is about actively engaging with life, being open to experiences, and daring to explore the uncharted territories within oneself. By doing so, individuals can unravel the layers of their inner ally or hero and embark on a continuous journey of self-discovery and growth.

DAY 9

Thoomani Maadalthil

Spiritual Lethargy

"O dear uncle's daughter! Your eyes are heavy in slumber in your highly decorated and beautiful chamber ornamented with

finery and pearls. Beautiful lamps around you burn with soft lights, and the fragrant incense wafts toward your comfortable bed. We implore you to open the latch of the bejeweled door. Dear Aunt, is your daughter bereft of speech, or has she lost the sense of hearing? Is she that lethargic? Or is there a gigantic spell she's under?" The great Magician/enchanter Madhava (another name for Vishnu) resides in Vaikunta. Oh, cousin! Call him by his several characters; only He can liberate you from this worldly trance."

P*O*E*M Exercise

P (Poem): The poem evokes the idea that there is a tussle within us to connect to the higher spirit when lured by temporary delights. A rested nature is not a result of indolence and indulgence. On the contrary, the desire for spiritual awakening comes only when the individual is open and willing to see beyond the smoke and mirrors of transitory pleasures. The girl has decorated her chamber with materials that cater to all senses. She has opened a treasure trove with textures, perfumes, and soft lights. Yet, she lingers in bed, unable to open her eyes to the sixth sense.

O (Observation):

You notice there's a sort of spiritual lethargy settling in – moments where all your given senses aren't fully engaged. A shiny distraction crosses your path, and suddenly, your duties fade into the background as you indulge in the allure. It's like your sense organs aren't being used judiciously towards duty.

There are times when things are taken for granted and overlooked, and the needs of both self and others are ignored due to preoccupations. The poet gently nudges, encouraging you to always keep that spiritual eye wide-open to remain mindful and engaged in the present, appreciating the richness of every moment without succumbing to distractions that lead to regret.

E (Engagement):

In the contemporary context, the poem serves as a metaphor for the ongoing struggle between the immediate allure of digital distractions and the more profound fulfillment that arises from spiritual self-reflection. The adorned chamber becomes symbolic of the captivating world of smartphones, social media, and other modern indulgences that, while tempting our senses, often lead to a sense of spiritual emptiness.

Amid a cold and rainy day, the cozy bed covers beckon, tempting you to stay within their comfort. Despite having set goals for the day, the faithful alarm chime fills you with a desire to retreat further into the warmth. Your body is rested, and wakefulness surrounds you, creating a mental battle as your mind rationalizes staying within the coziness. Giving in slightly, your thoughts start to meander, leading you down paths of fear, discomfort, and unproductive musings about others, colored by judgment, and irritation.

Ultimately, a moment of clarity breaks through. Casting off the covers, you choose to embrace the day. A refreshing shower, the infusion of natural light through open windows, and a conscious effort to gather your creative energy propel you to fulfill your daily duties. The poem thus encapsulates the struggle against the allure of perceived comfort and distraction, urging a conscious choice for a more purposeful and spiritually fulfilling path.

M (Movement):

Opting against the allure of idleness, wasteful ruminations, and the cozy covers, there's a conscious choice for active mindfulness. Heightened awareness of your senses becomes a tool for self-care and the care of others. This enhanced mindfulness becomes a catalyst for increased creativity, infusing joy into your work. Gratitude is expressed to a higher power, recognizing the unique spark that emerges when channeling a greater influence in your endeavors.

This mindful approach extends to the daily preparation of food, where the elevated awareness amplifies the taste and enjoyment of the culinary experience. Words and thoughts too, when infused with a connection to the Divine, take on a kinder, and more patient tone. Thoughtful actions, guided by this mindfulness, reverberate positively with those who cross your path. Embracing this mindset, there's a realization that what is put out into the universe returns in multiplicity, creating a harmonious cycle of positive energy and abundance.

DAY 10

Notru Chuvargam

Vanquish Slumber!

"Oh, my dear girl! We perform this vow to enter a higher realm. Why don't you open the doors or respond to our repeated knocks? Why is there this silence from you? Does the tulasi herb garland not remind you of His fragrant hair? He is praised for his courage and virtue, the one who grants us the divine drum. Do you remember the day when He vanquished the demon, Kumbakarna? Has he

gifted the grand sleep to you before the monster fell into the jaws of death? Oh, damsel! Understand you are a jewel among us. So overcome your sleep, open the doors to realize Him."

P*O*E*M Exercise

P (Poetry):

The poet's metaphorical knocking at the mind's door signifies the invitation to let the divine spirit enter, drawing an association between the Tulasi garland and the fragrance in the Divine's hair. The allusion to Kumbhakarna symbolizes the state of unawareness, emphasizing the importance of self-awareness to truly live rather than merely exist. The sleeping lass is likened to a jewel, highlighting the transformative power of self-awareness, much like polishing carbon into a sparkling diamond. This verse provides a gentle spiritual nudge.

O (Observation): The plant, a humble yet vital entity, becomes the focal point of the author's contemplation. Acknowledging its growth as a harmonious collaboration between soil, sunlight, and rain, the layers of self-awareness expand to include the hands of the planter whose care is intricately woven into the very fabric of the garland.

Following the intricate threads, the author reflects on the artistry of the herb garland, recognizing the weaver's stamp of craftsmanship. The fragrance, a delightful attribute, serves as a testament to the interconnected hand of nature.

The author ponders the profound question as to who put the fragrance in the holy basil, unveiling an awareness of the divine orchestrator behind the scenes. This spiritual journey unfolds a richer tapestry of gratitude, acknowledging the unique contributions of each element in the grand symphony of existence. This realization resonates with the inherent potential within to shine like a jewel, an integral part of the cosmic dance.

E (Engagement): In moments of complacency, perceptions can become akin to a deep slumber. Take, for instance, the common expectation of impeccable service in a restaurant merely due to the status of being a paying customer. However, with the lens of self-awareness, one has the capacity to transcend this lethargy and cultivate patience, consideration, and genuine appreciation for the service provided.

By infusing awareness into the present moment, the individual envisions themselves seated in a comfortable, climate-controlled space, gaining insight into the hard work undertaken by the kitchen staff to fulfill diverse orders under intense conditions. This heightened awareness prompts a shift in perspective—a departure from entitlement towards a profound acknowledgment of the shared human experience.

Expressing gratitude through small acts, such as a kind acknowledgment or a generous tip, becomes a deliberate choice. These actions not only elevate the personal dining experience but also serve as recognition of the interconnectedness of all involved. Furthermore, attributing this elevated experience to a higher force adds a layer of spiritual depth, fostering a harmonious exchange that extends beyond the transactional nature of a restaurant visit.

M (Movement): Engaging in a spiritual exercise for self-awareness brings forth a better version of self. The narrator places the bread she baked on the table. It's not just a loaf of bread; upon observation, it represents the giving earth, the sun, the soil, the rains, the hard-working farmers, and the people who brought the raw materials to her. It also embodies the individual who utilized these gifts to create bread for self and others. She can be part of this chain! There is immense gratitude in both giving and receiving.

Recognizing the inherent potential in everyone to shine, the narrator emphasizes the transformative power of infusing brilliance into their work. Drawing a parallel to a jeweler polishing a stone into a diamond, this energy elevates ordinary happiness to divine bliss. The acknowledgment of unlimited creativity as a divine birthright becomes a force that nourishes both oneself and others. This daily alchemy ensures that the ordinary is transmuted into the divine, creating a continuous cycle of inspiration and nourishment.

DAY 11

Katru Karavai

Break out of the Trance

"Slender lass, like a golden creeper, you have the mount of Venus, sensual like a hood of a cobra. You are blessed with the beauty of a forest peacock. Why must you still sleep?

You come from a lineage of mistresses who endlessly milk herds of fertile cows with never-ending milk flow. You come from the origin of the strong one who weakens and erases enemies without even going to war. O, the Flawless One, we know him as Govinda or the king of cowherds.

Arise and join your relatives and girlfriends; we're gathered here in your inner courtyard. We sing and take the name of the One who resembles the dark rain clouds, our Mugilvannan. You're blessed with great wealth, yet you insist on being in such a deep trance that you neither stir nor speak."

P*O*E*M Exercise

Poetry

P (Poetry): The poet, in describing the girl's sleep, alludes to a trance-like quality. Despite the girl being blessed with beauty, sensuality, and material riches, she is oblivious to gratitude. The poem introduces an awareness of the temporal, origin, relevance, and importance of these gifts, adding depth to the quest. It emphasizes the grace in enjoying these gifts and warns against defining oneself through transient qualities that may fade into oblivion. The verses acknowledge the enjoyment of attributes like sensuality, material prosperity, power, and charm, gaining depth when recognized in the context of their temporality and the permanence of spiritual divinity. When sensuality is conjoined with the spiritual, there is an infinite richness.

O (Observation): Life lacks a fixed map, and events beyond one's control can alter the known course. The poem serves as a guide for navigating life's ups and downs, emphasizing the spirit as a constant or permanent force. In a way, infusing the divine in enjoyment makes one enjoy each moment of the "now," despite oscillations. The awareness of the fleeting nature of joy and sorrow becomes a key tool for facing life's challenges.

Living in the present can be a source of permanent joy when one cultivates a mindset that appreciates the richness of each moment.

E (Engagement): Personal experiences of witnessing the impermanence of physical beauty, strength, and wealth resonate with the poet's observations. The importance of investing faith in the everlasting spirit is highlighted to enjoy life's fluctuations with strength and grace. Gratitude for gifts during joyful times is encouraged without letting them define one's identity. Sharing joy with others becomes a way to acknowledge the grace that placed those gifts at one's doorstep. Differentiating between the constant and the inconstant prepares for the inevitable downturns in life, fostering forbearance, and patience.

Imagine a successful professional in a corporate career, recognized for their intelligence, charm, and financial success. They navigate through life with confidence, enjoying the material comforts, and societal recognition that come with their achievements.

However, life is unpredictable, and external factors such as economic downturns or changes in the industry can impact their career. The charm that once opened doors may face challenges, and financial success may fluctuate. If this individual solely identifies with these external attributes, the shifts in their circumstances might lead to a crisis of identity and purpose.

In facing these challenges, the person can draw strength from recognizing the impermanence of external markers of success. By investing in qualities like resilience, adaptability, inner growth, and strong community ties, they build a foundation that remains steadfast despite external fluctuations.

M (Movement):

The poet's verse of the day highlights how living in the here and now contributes to lasting joy.

Mindfulness and Awareness: Being fully present in the current moment involves mindfulness and awareness. By paying attention to your thoughts, feelings, and surroundings without judgment, you can experience a deep sense of connection to the present. This awareness allows you to appreciate the beauty and simplicity of each moment.

Gratitude Practice: Focusing on the present encourages gratitude for what you have at the moment. Cultivating a daily gratitude practice, where you consciously acknowledge, and appreciate the positive aspects of your life, can contribute to a lasting sense of joy.

Acceptance of Impermanence: Understanding and accepting the impermanent nature of life can bring a sense of liberation. When you let go of attachments to outcomes or expectations, you free yourself from anxiety about the future or regrets about the past. Embracing the ebb and flow of life allows for a more profound experience of joy.

Connection with Others: Meaningful connections with others often happen in the present moment. When you fully engage in conversations, share experiences, and appreciate the people around you, you build deep, and lasting connections. These connections become a constant source of joy in your life.

Engagement in Flow Activities: Engaging in activities that bring you into a state of flow—where you are fully absorbed and focused—can be a pathway to permanent joy. This could be a creative pursuit, a hobby, or any activity that aligns with your passions and allows you to lose track of time.

Mindful Enjoyment of Pleasures: Whether it's savoring a delicious meal, enjoying nature, or relishing a moment of relaxation, being fully present amplifies the joy derived from life's simple pleasures. Mindful enjoyment allows you to extract maximum satisfaction from these experiences.

Living Your Values: Aligning your actions with dharmic core values and focusing on what truly matters to you brings a sense of purpose and fulfillment. When you live authentically in the present moment, your life becomes a reflection of your values, contributing to a deeper, and more lasting joy.

Cultivating Inner Peace: Living in the present often involves letting go of unnecessary worries and regrets. Practices such as meditation and mindfulness can help cultivate inner peace, creating a foundation for a sustained sense of joy regardless of external circumstances.

In essence, living in the present involves a conscious choice to embrace and fully experience each moment. By doing so, you build a reservoir of joy that is not dependent on external conditions but arises from your capacity to be present and engaged with life.

DAY 12

Kanaithilam Katrerumai

Willingness and Resistance

"The mother buffalo instinctively senses her hungry calf, and swollen udders release copious milk with no resistance. Prosperous sister! You own such a willing creature. Her abundant outpouring has transformed the courtyard into sludgy earth. While the early morning fog cover drips, we stand in the cold, hanging on the threshold by your courtyard door. We sing about Him, who valiantly vanquished the enemy king from Lanka. Why don't you try opening your lips in His praise to experience the sweetness in your heart? We realize this sweetness and implore you to arise from your slumber. So why do you put up such resistance?"

P*O*E*M Exercise

P (Poetry): The poet weaves a garland of beautiful similes and metaphors, transporting the reader to a scene centuries ago while maintaining current relevance. The girl, adorned with prosperity, remains nestled within the comfort of her bed covers as fog drips outside. Her willing friends implore her to awaken to the sweetness they seek. The poet employs the narrative of Lord Rama vanquishing the ten-headed demon as a figure of speech to overcome the reluctance preventing the girl from awakening her spirit. While sleep is restorative, indulging in it at the cost of everything else is portrayed as detrimental. The image of the mother buffalo outpouring copious milk at the mere thought of her calves hints at abundance, emphasizing trust in the One who provides. Further, the contrast between the cow's willingness with the girl's resistance is beautifully portrayed.

O (Observation): The poet's words prompt reflection on the importance of mindfulness. The girl, surrounded by material wealth, utilizes it without restraint, yet remains unaware of how these gifts came to her. Placing significant importance on enjoyment, she seems oblivious to the impermanence of these pleasures. The poem raises questions about the completeness of a prosperous life and the necessity of openness and willingness in one's quest for holistic well-being.

E (Engagement): There are moments of reluctance in the narrator when temporary comforts and delayed actions on duties cloud judgment. The speaker acknowledges instances of getting accustomed to privileges, neglecting empathy, and self-awareness, leading to a sense of entitlement over humility and gratitude. Additionally, there is a recognized unwillingness to let go of preconceived notions, symbolized as blanket covers hindering inner growth.

M (Movement):

The narrator's contribution for the day is framed as an affirmation list:

Motivation to dispel the fog preventing the inner divinity from sparkling.

Cultivation of awareness towards the received gifts.

Openness to alternative perspectives.

Recognition of the inherent ability to make a positive difference.

Utilization of personal abilities to strive for improvement.

Trusting in the universe by showing up despite perceived discomfort, leading to potential opportunities, or acceptance without expectations.

DAY 13

Pullinvai Keendanai

The Light and Shadow

"We gather here, and as we try to get closer to our goal, we sing in praise of the Valiant One. The Almighty vanquished the demon, who assumed the massive heron-like form, by ripping the beak open. He destroyed the evil Ravana and similar ogres as if it were child's play. Venus has arisen this early morn, and Jupiter has vanished from the sky. O beautiful girl, you with doe-eyes rimmed red like a flower, do you not hear the busy birds twitter? What makes you ignore our heartfelt call to dip in the cool, cleansing water? Why do you pretend to sleep? Quit your game to join us in completing this vow."

P*O*E*M Exercise

P (Poetry): The poet skillfully employs metanarrative in this verse, using two symbolic birds from different epics to represent opposing forces within us. Jatayu, the brave, and noble bird from the Ramayana, embodies the light within, fighting valiantly for justice. In contrast, Bakasura, the evil demon from the Mahabharata, represents the shadow that hinders our spiritual ascent.

The girl in the poem embodies reluctance and a lack of responsiveness, feigning ignorance of the world outside and exhibiting a streak of selfishness. The concept of war is touched upon through Jatayu's just fight to save the noble Sita.

O (Observation): The O in observation is related to Openness in this verse. One must open their heart and mind and express willingness to receive the Divine grace. The young girl is mired in comfort, unwilling to listen or respond to her friends inviting her, and pretends she does not hear them. Her behavior demonstrates a streak of selfishness. She knows the others wait for her response, unlike in other verses where the other girls are ignorant or deeply asleep.

The poet also touches upon the concept of just war. Jatayu, while trying to save Sita from the aggressor Ravana, chose to fight the just war. However, the evil Bakasura perpetrates the unjust war in another epic.

E (Engagement): The dominant idea that comes to mind is the human nature of not appreciating infinite gifts. Mother Earth is our greatest giver, and most humans treat her with attitudes of entitlement, disrespect, and abuse. We should be better stewards of the planet, yet our consumption of all things material grows exponentially, and we do not extend the use of our resources or recycle more. Instead, we continue to buy stuff with extra packaging and pollute the planet in every form possible. We know we're doing this, but are we willing to break through our comfortable cocoon? Instead, we pretend not to see the signs, even if they are right in front of us.

M (Movement): The movement aspect intricately explores the perpetual internal struggle between positive and negative impulses, underscoring the continuous choices that shape our daily lives. The poet highlights the significance of these choices, emphasizing that they not only define our character but also direct the course of our spiritual journey. Whether it involves resisting the allure of indulgence or opting for patience and kindness instead of negativity, these decisions contribute to the overall trajectory of our lives. The poet extends this idea beyond personal interactions to encompass broader themes such as how we treat others and our planet.

Additionally, the concept of alignment with belligerence or engaging in a just fight serves as a metaphor for the ethical battles we face, urging us to consider the moral implications of our actions in the larger context of our spiritual evolution.

DAY 14

Ungal Puzhakadai

The Backyard Pond

"In the pond of your own backyard, the red flowers are in full bloom. But, those night-blooming water lilies have closed their petals firm, don't you even see?

With white teeth, the sages in their brick-colored clothing depart to the temple to blow their conches. You are the illumined motivator in waking us up with the Mighty One's praises.

You're Nangai, the one with good qualities. Don't you feel guilty for having such a tongue? First, you tell us to awaken while you're beginning to slumber. Now we remind you to truly wake up.

Continue to sing the praises of the Lotus-eyed One who holds the white conch and the brilliant discus with ease in either hand."

P*O*E*M Exercise

P (Poetry):

The central theme of the poem centers on the concept of receptivity. The girls express their eagerness to open like lotuses to the sun, symbolizing their readiness to embrace the divine. However, they perceive a disconnection with the poet, who is likened to the night lily, implying a lack of openness or alignment. The poet also addresses leadership accountability.

O (Observation):

The girls, in their enthusiasm for spiritual growth, feel that the poet is not keeping pace with their eagerness to open. They sense a shift in focus away from self-discovery and remind the poet to truly wake up. Despite this, the poet remains dedicated to guiding others, albeit at a different pace.

E (Engagement):

The exercise of leadership involves receiving critique and adjusting methods for the greater good. While the poet has successfully elevated her friends, some are becoming impatient. Balancing methods and incorporating creativity without letting ego hinder progress becomes essential to maintain the overall rise in divinity levels.

M (Movement):

In the broader context, shedding ego becomes a crucial aspect of leadership, allowing the leader to adapt to others' needs. The ability to listen and adjust methods accordingly is viewed as an art, emphasizing the dynamic nature of the bigger picture in the journey towards spiritual growth.

DAY 15

Yelle Ilankiliye

A Conversation

Group: "Young lady, as beautiful as a colorful parrot, are you still languishing in bed?"

Girl: "Oh girls, you're shrill in speech. I will come, but it will be on my own time. (terms)"

Group: "Commendable are those clever words, but we can see through them. You're prevaricating."

Girl: "Well then, you have admirable traits, and I need to be left alone."

Group: "Why must it be different for you? Make haste and join us."

Girl: "Has everyone then set out?"

Group: "Yes, everyone has departed, and is assembling for the vow. Come outside, grace us with your presence, and honor us by taking a head count. Awaken, and sing along with us about the single-minded one who vanquished the gigantic, hostile elephant Kuvalayapida. Join us when we praise Him. He's the one who can remove the negative feelings from enemies. Come, let's complete our vow in honor of this exalted enchanter."

P*O*E*M Exercise

P (Poetry): The poet employs a conversational device of mutual dialog to illuminate the theme of ego in independence. While celebrating an independent spirit is commendable, the poem delves into the pitfalls of ego—attributing success solely to one's efforts and presuming omniscience while there is much yet to be explored.

The central theme revolves around the girl, who, although on a quest, has not fully recognized the collaborative nature of success. The narrative draws parallels with the mighty elephant Kuvalayapida, driven by ego, and rage to destroy Krishna under the influence of the malevolent Kamsa. However, when confronted with Krishna's courage and strategy, the elephant comprehends the toxic effects of rage and is vanquished once and for all, as its strength was used for hostile purposes.

The poet likens ego to a drunken elephant, emphasizing its uncontrolled, and destructive nature. This metaphor underscores the importance of humility, acknowledging the contributions of others, and remaining open to continuous learning on the quest for true wisdom.

O (Observation):

The observation highlights the concepts of humility, and collective action while emphasizing the need to open one's heart and mind to receive divine grace. Unlike in other verses where ignorance or deep sleep characterizes individuals, the young girl is portrayed as knowingly ignoring her friends' invitations, displaying a conscious choice of conceited selfishness.

At this stage, the energy to seek divinity has increased by leaps and bounds. Overcoming limiting obstacles requires tapping into the collective mindset's exponential energy. The conversational verse becomes an invitation from the group and self-permission for the girl to join something significantly more profound than her own knowledge in the quest for the Divine.

E (Engagement):

Emotions, as energy, transform lives at an atomic level. The analogy of quantum energy, with particles existing in a vacuum of invisible energy, parallels the transformative power of emotions. Choosing peaceful emotions transforms the mind, akin to the drunk elephant releasing grudges. The hindrance of ego to self-awareness obstructs genuine connections.

Sam, a person armed with prestigious degrees, prided himself on his intellectual prowess and dismissed wisdom lacking scholarly endorsement. Arrogant and shrill, he engaged in heated debates, waving away counsel with a figurative intellectual scepter. When a layman's wise advice challenged Sam's beliefs, he retorted, "I have the degrees; I know what I'm talking about."

As days passed, Sam's unwavering confidence resembled the raging elephant Kuvalayapida, charging ahead fueled by arrogance. Despite these, his work was mediocre at best. A mentor intervened, saying, "Your degrees are tools, not weapons of ego. Wisdom lies in listening and learning." Sam, in a metaphorical debate, realized his ego was that incontrollable elephant needing taming. Joining a collective project, he embraced humility. Through shared endeavor Sam embarked on a journey of enlightenment, realizing true wisdom is shared, and knowledge amplifies through honoring multiple viewpoints. His work seen through other eyes attained depth and dimensions that he had not foreseen. Sam learned to navigate the tumultuous waters of intellectual arrogance toward the serene shores of shared wisdom and unity.

This modern example emphasizes the transformative power of humility, benevolent speech, active listening, respecting multiple perspectives, and collective action in overcoming ego.

Movement

Navigating life with an individualistic approach has its merits, yet moments of error arise from ignoring well-meaning advice. Being the loudest voice may silence the wisdom in others. The strength of creative beings multiplies in like-minded company. Embracing diverse perspectives fosters exponential growth. In the vast ocean of samsara, rowing together turns the journey into the destination, while rowing alone in the absence of group unison can be daunting.

The author realizes rowing together and rowing alone depends on the circumstances, goals, and the individual's preferences. A harmonious balance between both approaches may provide a well-rounded and fulfilling journey through life's waters.

DAY 16

Nayakanai Nindra

The Gatekeeper

"O Nayaka of the palace of our leader Nanda Gopa, you stand guard at the door with flags and festoons. Kindly open the latch of the decorated door with bells. We are only young, innocent devotees from unlettered cowherd homes.

Yesterday, Mannivanan the Enchanter verbally promised his protection. He will give us the small beating drums to perform our vow. After purification of mind, body, and spirit, we have only come to wake Him gently out of slumber with our songs. Please do not deny us entry by telling us to move away. Instead, please undo the locked doors to provide us access."

P*O*E*M Exercise

The narrator recognizes the pivotal moment in the girls' journey as they stand before *Nayaka*, the guard at the door to the divine abode. This interaction becomes a symbolic checkpoint, testing the sincerity, and authenticity of the seekers. Despite their humble backgrounds, the girls exhibit profound understanding and faith in their mission to awaken the Divine through their pure intentions.

P (Poetry): The girls, with earnestness, and sincerity, stand before the door guarded by Nayaka. Their innocent hearts beat in rhythm with the anticipation of the Divine encounter. The door is adorned with flags and festoons, and they request the *Nayaka* to open it, inviting them to step closer to the heart of the divine abode.

In their plea to the guard, the girls express their simplicity and humility. They acknowledge their young age and the humble backgrounds from which they come. Despite the apparent lack of sophistication, they hold the promise of Mannivanan, the precious Enchanter, who has verbally assured them protection and provided small beating drums for their sacred vow. This mention adds a layer of trust and faith to their quest. He is the bridge between the ordinary and the divine, offering support, and encouragement to these young devotees. Their purpose is clear – to purify mind, body, and spirit, and gently wake the Divine from slumber with their soulful songs.

O (Observation): The interaction with Nayaka becomes a pivotal moment in their journey. The guard serves as a metaphorical checkpoint, testing the authenticity, and readiness of the seekers. The girls, undeterred by their simple origins, demonstrate a profound understanding of their mission and the significance of their devotion. The *Parai* or drum as the girls think it, now beats for higher consciousness.

E (Engagement): This stage of the journey emphasizes the importance of trust and faith. The girls believe in the Enchanter's promise, and they exhibit faith in their ability to awaken the Divine through their pure intentions. It reflects a universal truth – the journey towards the divine is not determined by external appearances or worldly status, but by the sincerity, and authenticity of one's spiritual quest.

M (Movement): As the narrator reflects on this phase of the journey, she is reminded of the moments in her own life when faith and trust played crucial roles; the times when she had to stand before metaphorical doors, unsure of what lay beyond. This prompts the narrator to question the intruders encountered in their spiritual journey – the doubts, fears, and uncertainties. Can the narrator, like the girls, stand with sincerity, and trust, ready to open the doors to deeper spiritual understanding? The *Nayaka's* role as a guard raises questions about the intruders in her life – those who challenge her and test her resolve.

In the ocean of spiritual exploration, each interaction, each guard, and each door present an opportunity for growth. It involves trusting the self, the process, and the universe. It's not merely about reaching a destination; it's about the transformation that occurs along the way. The *Nayaka* within us stands not as an obstacle but as a guide, steering towards a deeper realization of the highest potential.

DAY 17

Ambarame Thaneere

Charity in Thought, Word, and Deed

"O Nandagopa, the father of my Lord, you are the philanthropic doer of good deeds. You generously donate clothing, water, and food to others. Please wake up!

Oh, Yashoda, you're the illumined lamp, a beacon for all the slender women from the cowherd family. Please wake up.

O blessed brother Baladeva; you sleep with the golden anklet manifesting your prosperity.

O Krishna! As Vishnu, the mighty king of Lords, you assumed an extraordinary form and tore up the sky to measure the earth. (Referring to Vamana Avatar)

O Balarama, we implore you to arise with your younger brother Krishna."

P*O*E*M Exercise

P (Poetry):

The verses weave a tapestry of reverence, addressing Nandagopa, Yashoda, Baladeva, and Krishna with profound devotion. The poet employs rich metaphors to evoke the divine qualities within each figure, portraying Nandagopa as a benevolent donor, Yashoda as an illumined lamp of wisdom, Baladeva as a symbol of prosperity, and Krishna as the mighty king of Lords.

O (Observation): The poet's invocation highlights the multifaceted nature of divinity, encompassing generosity, wisdom, prosperity, and omnipotence. The use of vivid imagery adds depth to the spiritual narrative, inviting readers to contemplate the symbolic significance of each addressed figure in the context of their own spiritual journey.

E (Engagement): This stage of the poetic journey prompts reflection on the diverse aspects of the divine within and around us. It encourages an exploration of generosity, wisdom, prosperity, and strength as integral components of a holistic spiritual awakening. By acknowledging and aspiring to embody these qualities, individuals may deepen their connection to the divine within.

M (Movement): Inspired by the verses, one might embark on a personal journey of self-discovery and spiritual growth. This could involve acts of generosity, seeking wisdom from enlightened sources, cultivating prosperity in various dimensions of life, and recognizing inner strength. The awakening becomes not merely a call to consciousness but an active engagement with the divine attributes that resonate with the spiritual seeker.

As the poetic voyage continues, the unfolding verses carry the anticipation of a profound awakening, urging the reader to explore the richness of divine qualities within the tapestry of their own existence.

Let's consider a modern-day scenario that reflects the qualities of generosity, wisdom, prosperity, and strength in a small incident:

Imagine a young professional named Maya who works in Boston. One day, she notices a homeless person sitting outside a coffee and donut shop, shivering in the cold. As a policy, the donut shop does not permit access to nonpaying customers. Touched by compassion, Maya decides to act.

Generosity: Inspired by the spirit of Nandagopa, known for his generosity, Maya buys a hot meal and a bottle of water for the homeless person. For that moment, the homeless individual is warm and fed. Her act of generosity goes beyond a simple donation; it reflects a genuine desire to make a positive impact on someone's life.

Wisdom: Channeling the wisdom attributed to Yashoda who is compared to the illumined lamp, Maya doesn't just provide material support. She engages the homeless person in conversation, seeking to understand his story and challenges. This wisdom allows her to offer not just immediate assistance but also empathy and understanding.

Prosperity: Baladeva, associated with prosperity, represents more than material wealth. In Maya's case, prosperity is manifested in her willingness to share her knowledge and resources. She informs the homeless person about local shelters, support services, and job assistance programs, aiming to contribute to his overall well-being.

Strength: Drawing inspiration from Krishna's might, Maya displays inner strength. She doesn't shy away from addressing the issue at hand, taking proactive steps to help someone in need. Her strength lies not only in physical actions but also in the courage to confront societal challenges and advocate for positive change.

DAY 18

Undu Madagalitran

The Influencer

"O daughter-in-law of the brave Nandagopala who conquered several rutting elephants, please wake up. Roosters crow loudly everywhere, and the cuckoos flock on the jasmine trellises, sing, and wake us up.

Oh, lady! You're the one with lustrous tresses scented with sandalwood; please be kind and open the door! You have hands like a delicate pink lotus, yet you play the Supreme Lord like a ball. We would also like to joyfully sing with you your Lover's praises. So let the stacked bracelets jingle musically as you open the door with those petal-soft hands to let us in."

P*O*E*M Exercise

P (Poetry): The girls fervently implore the divine consort, likening their effort to the resounding calls of roosters and cuckoos that awaken. The poet draws an analogy with playing ball, where the person in control of the ball influences its movement. Similarly, the feminine consort holds significant sway over the Supreme. The plea is for her to open the door, allowing them closer to the Divine. Feminine energy, representing compassion, empathy, and influence, is emphasized. Despite the Omnipotent battlefield prowess, the poet portrays Him as pliable in the face of her heart. The girls appeal to her understanding, expressing their willingness to draw nearer and beseech for spiritual access.

O (Observation): The observation underscores the fusion of *Daya*, or Compassion, with the Goddess Lakshmi in the Lord's heart. The Lord remains incomplete without her, and no amount of valor, might, or power can compensate for the absence of compassion.

The philosophical point recognizes that opposing forces are interdependent and complementary. It's not about the absence of compassion or other qualities in one gender; rather, it emphasizes the harmonious balance and interplay of these forces to create a unified whole. Both masculine and feminine energies contribute unique strengths, and their synthesis leads to a more complete and holistic existence. In the context of the poem, the acknowledgment of feminine energy doesn't diminish the importance of masculine qualities but highlights the synergy needed for spiritual completeness.

E (Engagement): To embody divinity, one must internalize the qualities of the Divine. While the Omnipotent is mighty and brave, the fusion with the goddess of compassion elevates him to the status of the Supreme.

M (Movement): The poem inspires a compassionate approach in undertaking any endeavor for oneself and others. While possessing individual traits, opportunities, and the willingness to progress, it emphasizes the importance of incorporating understanding and seeking support from compassionate individuals. The balance of male and female energy is crucial to completeness. The poem underscores that only through compassion and empathy can the mighty transcend to become the Almighty. The author reflects on a personal experience where a lack of compassion in advice-giving led to hurt feelings and a missed opportunity to offer help in a more empathetic manner.

DAY 19

Kuttu Vilakeriya

The Bower

Oh, Nappinai, you have adorned your hair with bunches and heaps of fragrant flowers upon your lovely hair.

The gently burning oil lamp burns all around while you sleep on a luxuriously elevated bed with ivory posts. The cotton mattress upon which you climb is so comfortably soft."

Oh, broad-shouldered Lord! You close your eyes comfortably upon her generous breasts; why don't you speak?

Oh, beautiful Nappinai, with your kohl-ringed dark eyes, you've captivated Him. How much longer do you intend to keep him? He's glued to your charms and is oblivious to us. We see you cannot bear to be parted from him. Will you not release him even for a fraction of a second? Can't you see this is wrong? Does it befit you? We cannot accept this."

P*O*E*M Exercise

P (Poetry):

Although the bridal vow starts at the microcosm, it brings awareness that the spiritual path is expansive. With creative words, the poet weaves an image of a new bride languishing with her consort in a warm, softly-lit bower of love. The girls outside wait interminably in the fog to have a similar connection with the Divine. Immersed in love, the divine consort does not recognize the discomfort faced by the devotees shut out of such warmth. The wicks of the lamp burn slowly, reminding the new bride of her role as she enters a new home. They must remind her to cultivate, include, and maintain the love of the family. Are they not of the same kin? Where is her patience and empathy for others waiting in the cold? Where is the wisdom to understand the love shared? Is love augmented? The devotees wait to unite with the Supreme love, and such exclusivity is limiting. Nevertheless, they are resolute in their quest and seek the same qualities in Nappinai with these accountability questions. They gently chastise the Divine for surrendering to Nappinai's attention while ignoring all other seekers.

O (Observation): The bridal vow seeks to unite the yearning souls to the Divine groom. All creatures, regardless of gender, are the brides seeking to connect like soulmates. The love of the Divine is available for the entire universe, and locking it up, or not having access to it limits the brilliance of the devotees and the

Divine. Love has no limits, and it only increases exponentially with every connection.

E (Engagement): The poet has created a mood so prevalent with bridal mysticism. It implies a longing for connection, discovery, and fulfillment. The sensual aspect is an important aspect of one's fulfilled life. It also serves as a device that shows the yearning for a spiritual connection. There are many facets of existence, and romance is one. It serves as a vehicle to make devotees aware of spiritual hunger. In a young girl's life, the relevance of romance is high. However, when infused with divinity, these bridal vows create a more profound, respectful relationship between individuals.

M (Movement): The wicks on the bridal lamp represent inclusiveness, patience, caring, wisdom, resoluteness, and acting honorably. Incorporating the glow from these burning wicks in daily lives ushers in the elevated spirit.

Karina and Neil, newlyweds, arrive with their extended family and friends for a celebration thrown in their honor. Despite being immersed in their private cocoon of romance, they recognize the importance of extending their joy to the wider circle. Understanding the efforts made by family and friends to celebrate with them, they appreciate the shared happiness and acknowledge the significance of community in their joyous union.

In a philosophical sense, the scenario reflects the idea of engaging through the lens of inclusiveness, empathy, and the recognition of a broader community beyond one's beloved immediate circle.

DAY 20

Mupattu Muvar

Sleeping Supreme

"O Valiant Sri Krishna, you are of immeasurable strength, a leader, savior, and protector of three hundred thirty million devas; please wake up from your slumber for us. Even before they sought succor from you, you remained omnipresent for demigods. You helped prevent any harm even before it came their way. O Powerful One, only you can obstruct, or remove any fear.

Please arise and wake. O impartial and honest One! You are the one with the immense strength to protect the devotees. You inflict sorrow on the enemies impartially. O Pure one, we entreat you to wake up to provide us the same protection you provide to the devas.

O consort Nappinai, you lie beside Him with tender breasts resembling golden cones. With your coral lips(mouth)and slender hips, you embody the Ultimate Woman, Lakshmi (Periya Piratti), in every way. Please wake up! Gently rouse your husband with the fan and give him the mirror. Permit him to bathe with us in the shower of his mercy!"

P*O*E*M Exercise

P (Poetry):

The damsels persist in their attempt to awaken the spirit and his consort. One without the other is not complete. They go back and forth between mighty strength and compassion in their appeal. They ask for the opportunity to serve them.

O (Observation): The devotees awaken compassion first by appealing to Nappinai. Then, they ask for the opportunity to serve with the fan and the mirror in how she services the Divine. The fan cools people around, providing comfort. The mirror reflects the beauty of the spirit. One can emulate the same by remembering the Divine.

E (Engagement):

How does one incorporate a divine spirit into daily life? As the fan provides a comforting breeze on a hot day, we can serve ourselves, and others. How can we emulate the divine? Mirroring positive behavior helps make a better version of self. The reflecting aspect of a mirror provides better observation of flaws in self. The lack of absorption in a mirror allows for rejecting those undesirable qualities through introspection. If the mirror reflects the world's deficiencies, it is an opportunity to understand the temporality of it all. The mirror is tied neither to joy nor sorrow.

M (Movement):

This verse motivates the speaker further to incorporate compassion into her daily life. She feels compelled to be kinder to herself as well as to others around her. Infusing service with the heart becomes another way for her to connect with the higher spirit. Recognizing that she possesses the necessary skillset and tools to accomplish tasks reminds her to be grateful. Despite moments of forgetfulness, ego-driven reactions, and feelings of entitlement, she can use the mirror as a mental device to reflect positivity seen elsewhere. This practice helps her transition from a state of self-absorption to self-awareness. When she executes tasks with compassion, the job becomes enjoyable, and the results often have an extra something to them. Today, when she engages in any activity, she plans to mirror the kindness someone has shown her with mindful compassion.

One day, while driving her car, another driver on the road repeatedly made gestures that initially irritated her. His pointing fingers, mouthing words, and sounding horn got to her. However, she decided to be calm instead of reacting with anger, choosing to stay composed. The other driver continued to engage, and eventually, she realized he was trying to convey something important. It turns out that the expensive long scarf she wore was caught in the car door, flapping outside, collecting dust, and posing a safety risk. This experience taught her the importance of resisting impulsive reactions, as sometimes, what may seem like rudeness could be an attempt to help. The other driver could have ignored the situation, as it was not his problem, but he chose to help instead. Misinterpretations often arise from a self-absorbed perspective, clouding understanding of others' intentions. A calm and open mind allows the speaker to see situations for what they truly are, fostering better understanding, and avoiding unnecessary conflicts.

DAY 21

Yetra Kalangal

Impartial Grace

"Abundant milk flows incessantly from the fantastic udders of the solid and healthy cows. The pails cannot contain such abundance, so the milk runs all over.

O Son of the accomplished Nandagopa! Please awaken! The supreme texts refer to you as Omnipotent. Please make your glory visible to us, simple cowherds, in a fashion we can also understand. Oh, Supreme Lord! You show yourself to your devotees in various ways. Oh, glowing beacon! We entreat you to wake up for us.

Even your enemies surrender at your feet with realization. That action alone is a victory from the pain of enmity. You are their final refuge when they come helpless at your feet. Indeed, can you not conquer over us, simple lasses? We come to your doorstep with nothing but devotion. We aim to laud your glory and surrender in love to you completely."

P*O*E*M Exercise

P (Poetry):

The poet references the avatar of Krishna, who appeals to the divinity in all through love. He is the epitome of love and the creator behind Vedas and Upanishads. Yet, He's the one who goes beyond these scriptures and can easily be attained. Metaphorically, she implies the need for the Divine to shower grace like cows with abundant milk. It is a symbiotic relationship, as the pots placed under the willing udders overflow. If a pail with the ability to hold the ocean is placed under the udders, the abundant milk still cannot be contained. Such is the outpouring of divine grace to the ones who are benefactors. When the girls question why there is a withholding of this grace when they come with love, they contrast the grace shown to enemies who surrender to love. This is the poet's way of highlighting that every person intending to follow the dharmic path of love is worthy of the Supreme grace. Her words reveal that the One is neither authoritarian nor vengeful. His devotees have a full right to question the disbursement of love.

O (Observation):

There are ways to connect to the Supreme. Some may think it is through rites and rituals, and others may think it is through scriptures, treatises, and knowledge. They may all be part of the exercise to understand multiple Supreme facets. But does that exclude simple folk like these cowherd lasses? Even formidable foes seeking surrender and atonement get access to Supreme glory, is the innocent devotion from these lasses not enough?

E (Engagement):

Are the girls indeed coming with love? They ask why the One showers grace to once inimical foes who surrender to love more generously than them. There's that smidgen of ego in understanding His mysteries. The journey continues even if the divine consort has become one with them.

At the very concrete level, one can infuse the qualities of the Divine to overcome obstacles within and beyond. This infusion of the spirit makes challenges surmountable. Here's a contrasting situation.

The narrative of Pal and Devi vividly illustrates the profound influence of mindset and reciprocity on individual journeys.

Mindset: Pal, with a petulant, and blaming mindset, tends to attribute his perceived lack of opportunities to external factors. This mindset limits his ownership of decisions, obstructs awareness of alternative opportunities, and fosters discontentment. Pal's focus on scarcity blinds him to the abundance that may exist in his life. On the contrary, Devi embodies a positive mindset. Despite facing challenges, she approaches life with gratitude and relentless effort. Her focus on growth and appreciation for the support provided by others enables her to navigate obstacles with resilience and openness to opportunities.

Reciprocity: The concept that what one puts out in the universe, one receives is highlighted through the stories of Pal and Devi. Pal, with a mindset centered on scarcity and blame, receives nothing in return. His negative approach limits the positive energy he attracts, hindering his progress, and closing doors. In contrast, Devi's positive mindset, and gratitude create a reciprocal flow of positive energy. She sees abundant choices, embraces her journey with resilience, and, as a result, doors open for her. The reciprocity of her positive energy contributes not only to her personal growth but also strengthens her relationships and expands her opportunities.

Impact on Journey and Outcomes: The stories of Pal and Devi underscore how one's perspective and approach to challenges significantly impact their journey and outcomes. Pal's mindset hampers his ability to recognize and capitalize on opportunities, leading to discontentment. Devi's positive mindset becomes a driving force, propelling her forward, fostering personal growth, and opening unforeseen doors. The contrast between Pal and Devi serves as a powerful reminder of the transformative potential embedded in one's mindset and the reciprocal nature of energy in shaping life's outcomes.

The narratives of Pal and Devi emphasize the importance of cultivating a positive mindset, practicing gratitude, and understanding the reciprocal relationship between one's outlook and the opportunities that unfold in their journey.

M (Movement):

In times of trouble, the speaker sometimes catches herself wondering, *"Why me?"* Despite being aware of the abundance and grace in her life, there are moments when the speaker falls into the trap of comparing her journey with others, assessing her efforts through a narrow prism. It's not a helpful mindset. In such moments, this verse inspires the speaker to shift her focus, urging her to channel more effort into reaching her destination instead of fixating on someone else's journey. The speaker has come to realize that the Divine never withholds grace from the devoted, and delays might be opportunities for a deeper assessment of her spiritual journey. This perspective encourages the speaker to appreciate her unique path, understanding that each step, even if delayed, contributes to the growth of her spirit.

DAY 22

Anganmanyalatu Arasar

Victory in Surrender

P*O*E*M Exercise

Like the once-proud kings in this beautiful world, we also surrender entirely to the foot of your reclining throne. We have destroyed all ego. Like them, we have come in a large group. We've come to the one who has triumphed over us with heads bowed, and we seek your refuge.

Will you not open your red, intense eyes ever so slowly to let us in your line of vision? Will you not open your eyes like little slits on a dancing bell while initially casting your eyes upon us? We plead that you gently open them wide, resembling red, fully bloomed lotuses. Only this way can we get used to the intensity of your powerful vision.

Let those intense eyes slowly unfurl with the gentle moon cooling the resplendent sun.

Please behold us. With your divine grace, all our mortal sorrows will completely disappear."

P*O*E*M Exercise

P (Poetry):

The imagery captures the thirst for Divine attention. The poet weaves such a beautiful garland of thought with this verse. In the prior verse, the tiny speck of ego the girls carried is shed, and the girls have surrendered to love. Love is inclusive, selfless, and a mighty collective force. The use of mighty kings coming in complete surrender to receive divinity represents the conquering of ego despite power, wealth, fame, and repute. The poetry of receiving divine grace bit by bit is well illustrated with a request of opening the divine eye like a slit on the dancing bell, preparing them to receive slowly until the eyes open like fully bloomed lotuses. This, the poet recommends, would be like a combination of the fiery sun and the cooling moon.

O (Observation):

There is an evolutionary shift in the dropping of ego. One must surrender to the divine way to get rid of mortal sorrows. One must be primed to receive divine grace. Not everyone is ready, and even if one is far along in the journey, the divine grace must be calibrated by the sender to the recipients who may not be ready to fully receive the majesty of such grace.

E (Engagement):

The lasting quality of divinity is well brought out here. The priceless quality of the immortal spirit is not measured by fame, power, or wealth. Separation from this grace in our daily lives will not satisfy the deep thirst within, even with infinite material comforts. A life blessed with divine grace is purposeful, meaningful, and satisfying.

M (Movement):

Attachment to material objects and ego gives grief. However, shedding the ego ultimately brings grace to the door. This is a challenging exercise even for a person with self-awareness.

Consider Jay's example as he takes on the responsibility of being the family provider very seriously. He once decided to invest a significant portion of his savings in the stock market with the hope of securing a better future for his family. Unfortunately, due to unforeseen economic downturns or market fluctuations, Jay faces a substantial financial loss.

Devastated by the failure of his financial endeavors and feeling personally responsible for providing for his family, Jay falls into a deep depression. He struggles with a sense of failure, unable to realize that his family does not judge him for his actions and remains supportive. His depression stems from an intense attachment to the material identity of being the family provider, highlighting the challenges individuals face when their self-worth becomes entangled with labels, they ascribe to themselves. He does not see this as an opportunity to be the resilient provider and is ashamed he has failed the family by not discharging the provider role. This scenario underscores the importance of maintaining a healthy perspective on material pursuits and finding intrinsic value beyond societal roles and counting other blessings like a solid family rooting for his well-being.

Maintaining self-awareness and a spiritual attitude is an ongoing journey, and the author transparently acknowledges moments of reacting with ego instead of wisdom. This higher spirit mirroring is highlighted as a continuous struggle, like the commitment required for physical exercise at the gym. The comparison emphasizes that just like physical fitness, spiritual fitness, and a more meaningful life require consistent effort and dedication. This recognition underscores the ongoing nature of the spiritual journey, emphasizing growth, and learning from both successes and challenges.

The poet skillfully employs the analogy of mighty kings humbly surrendering their ego to the Divine, raising the question of why everyday individuals struggle. This prompts contemplation on the human tendency to grapple with ego, perhaps stemming from attachment to identity, desires, or the material world. The contrast between the surrendered kings and common individuals invites reflection on the universal challenge of overcoming ego and embracing humility in the pursuit of spiritual growth.

VERSE 23

Mari Mazhai Muzhanjil

Hibernation

POEM Exercise

"Deep inside the dark mountain cave, the majestic lion lies with his mate during the wet, rainy season. Verily, O Lord, you are the epitome of such rousing majesty! So please come out of this hibernation for the sake of your eager devotees.

Acknowledge us with your wide-open, brilliant eyes. Those fiery eyes reassure us simultaneously with protection as gentle as the red flower petals.

Rise, stretch, and claim your surroundings! We only desire to see the splendor that you are.

As the lion spreads out the magnificent mane, it shakes it side to side, the hair bristles and crackles, and the majestic one roars resoundingly. We desire to see this leonine majesty in full glory.

O Enchanter with your violet hue of the Kayampoo flower! Be kind and emerge from your royal chamber. Walk our way like the majestic lion. Bless us with the vision of your regal gait as you ascend on a highly decorated, grand throne made for someone as glorious as you. Acknowledge us of our presence at your feet by enquiring why we are here before you."

P*O*E*M Exercise

P (Poetry):

The poet appeals to the paternal aspect of the Divine. Like cubs seeking affection, they come to Him for compassion and protection. His red eyes can be fiery towards enemies, while being softly compassionate as lotus petals to devotees.

O (Observation):

This is called *Vatsalya* or parental affection. Even a majestic lion displays the sentiment to the cubs keeping them safe and secure from enemies. We often talk about external enemies. By seeking protection and imitating the Divine, we can overcome them. However, are those the only enemies the poet refers to through these metaphors?

Enemies can reside within. They come as greed, sloth, lack of correct action, envy, covetousness, rage, and an unquenchable ego. However, with love for self and for others, one can overcome these enemies that impede our evolution to a higher self.

E (Engagement)

Imagine a scenario where individuals, instead of cultivating divine qualities, succumb to base instincts like greed, envy, and rage. This erosion of higher virtues in society has exponential consequences, jeopardizing the safety of the world. When leaders or individuals prioritize self-interest over collective well-being, conflicts escalate, and the world becomes an unsafe place for everyone. The absence of compassion and understanding, akin to the Divine's soft-petaled lotus gaze, leads to a deterioration of the moral fabric that ensures the safety and harmony of the world.

In navigating personal challenges, the author discovers inspiration in emulating the Divine when faced with difficult individuals or moments. For instance, she chooses to foster more patience in response to perceived threats, recognizing that miscommunication and misperception often underlie conflicts.

M (Movement):

Imagine you are part of a homeowners' association (HOA), and there's a disagreement about a community decision that directly impacts you. Despite expressing your concerns and attempting to reach a consensus, the situation remains unresolved, and your perspective is not being considered.

As a last resort, asserting yourself in this real-life scenario could involve:

Organizing a Meeting: Propose a meeting with the members of the homeowners' association to address the concerns openly. Clearly express your perspective and reasons behind your stance.

Gathering Support: Reach out to neighbors who share similar concerns and gather support for your position. A collective voice can be more influential in swaying decisions.

Presenting Alternatives: Offer viable alternatives or compromises that could address the concerns of all parties involved. This demonstrates a willingness to find common ground.

Seeking External Mediation: If internal discussions prove unproductive, consider seeking external mediation, or involving a neutral third party to help facilitate a resolution.

Public Awareness: In extreme cases, when the well-being of the community is at stake, you might choose to raise awareness publicly. This could involve communicating with local media or using social platforms to inform residents about the situation.

Asserting yourself in real-life situations often requires a combination of effective communication, collaboration, and, when necessary, taking strategic actions to protect your rights or the well-being of the community.

These times are particularly demanding, with the lingering effects of a pandemic causing job losses and upheaval, testing people's mental resilience. Instances of unwarranted rage and exploding meltdowns contribute to a world marked by division and intolerance.

When confronted with genuine external threats, it becomes imperative to apply wisdom in one's response. Just as the fiery lion rises to preserve dignity and safety as a last resort, there are moments in life that call for assertiveness and protection.

This verse underscores the importance of embodying divine qualities in all situations. Navigating escalating problems requires discernment to distinguish between the threat within, perceived threats, and real threats. Acting with the dignity of the lion, symbolic of the Divine, becomes crucial in maintaining balance and understanding. In doing so, individuals gain insight into the multifaceted qualities within the Divine.

DAY 24

Andru Ivulagam

Glory Be!

"Those praiseworthy feet once measured this entire earth. We're here to worship them today.

We laud and worship the fame with which you won over Ravana, the southern king of Lanka.

You saw through the ogre called Sakata, who came disguised as a hurtling cart about to wreak destruction on hapless innocents. We praise your valor in annihilating him.

You saw through another ogre Vatsasura who came disguised as a hapless calf. You cleverly destroyed another ogre Kapitasura who came disguised as a wood apple. They served as parts of a slingshot in destroying evil tendencies with one action."

We praise and worship your strength and intelligence in destroying both perpetrators simultaneously.

As a protector, you lifted an entire mountain, using it as an umbrella to shelter us from the storm.

We worship your compassion.

We hail the great spear you hold in your victorious hand that removes hostility.

We come here only to secure the gift of drums in submission, so we can sing your praises perpetually. Please show your compassionate nature and emancipate us.

P*O*E*M Exercise

P (Poetry):

The careful placement of the narrative highlights the interplay of light and dark. The Vamana Avatar incident serves to narrate the liberation of King Mahabali, who shed his ego in total generosity. Seizing Sita against her wishes, the covetous Ravana faced destruction by the Supreme in the avatar of Rama. Violent jealousy was nipped by the brave action of Krishna's avatar. Krishna annihilated hypocrisy by unmasking and destroying the deceitful demon that came disguised as a hapless calf. Krishna also used intelligence, valor, and uprightness to kill another monster. Protecting the people from enemies and natural disasters, he was around to lift an entire mountain as an umbrella for the people when the natural disaster struck. For these reasons, his devotees come in gratitude to hail the glory, and they laud his spear that removes hostility. Finally, they declare they have come to the Divine in complete faith to request the drums. Devotees seek to use them in rhythm as they sing glories in perpetuity. With sincerity, they seek divine compassion to emancipate them.

O (Observation):

Demons, monsters, triumph, and emancipation. What is the main idea in this verse? There is a divine order in life, and most cultures agree upon this. Using epics and narratives, one can better understand this concept. Referencing the Supreme's sterling qualities, one can imitate Him. Evil forces need not be external. They could also breed within. This is an easy device to nip those tendencies or stay away from them. One could cultivate the divine spirit with faith, compassion, and courage.

Submission can be a weakness if one bows down to tyranny or evil forces. Yet, it can elevate, liberate, and emancipate if one submits to divine qualities. If the One is a protector, does it include protection from hostile enemies? The poet's allusion in lauding the Divine hand holding the sharp spear is used for this reason. The spear removes the hostility from the root, and even once fearful foes have the privilege of protection and evolution. Embracing the divine qualities ensures the safety of one and all and the entire universe.

E (Engagement):

I am struck by the concept of warring for aggrandizement, resources, religion, and other ideologies. These are the negative qualities of the entire humankind. Instead, war needs to quell greed, jealousy, coveting, hypocrisy, falsehood, hostility, and hate, and replace them with an arsenal of divine qualities of protection and compassion. Second chances are always welcome, and once hostile foes can evolve into better beings.

M (Movement):

In personal movement, the commitment to staying on the dharmic path is acknowledged as challenging yet rewarding. Instances of impatience and frustration can be replaced with patience and compassion, and standing up for oneself against unkindness is seen as necessary without engaging in unnecessary conflict. This requires wisdom, intelligence, and patience akin to the divine, accessible to everyone.

Saru spent much time working endlessly on a project for months. She poured her soul into it. At the final presentation, Lana took all the credit for Saroo's hard work. This left Saroo feeling betrayed, helpless, and outraged.

Taking a deep breath, she shook out anger clouding her mind. She replaced victim mentality with a warrior mindset. Incorporating equipoise, she met with Lana and decided to adhere to her principles and integrity without impulsively lashing out. Saru respectfully addressed the issue. She handed out the copious proof of work she had done on the project, and requested there be a focused solution that honored professional integrity and the situation at hand.

Saru stood up for herself with a dharmic approach. This led to Lana realizing the fault of her selfish unprofessionalism. Lana then went a step further to rectify the issue by acknowledging Saru's immense contributions to the project in front of the whole team.

Fighting the good fight through integrity and honesty helps one navigate injustices with grace. It also earns the perceived foe's respect.

Not all the time can one expect results like this. However, standing up to injustice through a fair fight aligns with dharmic principles.

The poet advocates removing hostility from the root. In modern society, the prevalence of troll farms breeding toxicity and infighting, especially in the era of AI, poses a significant threat to global stability and harmony. The potential for malevolent actors to exploit AI for destructive purposes is a concern that could lead to chaos and jeopardize our existence. The concept of divinity in the daily is highlighted, emphasizing the idea that our actions in the world have repercussions, echoing the principle of what we put out into the universe returning to us manifold. By doing so, individuals can contribute to preserving, protecting, and honoring the multitude of blessings that exist in the world. The call is to foster a collective commitment to spiritual values, wisdom, kindness, and compassion, acting as a counterforce to the negative influences that may arise from the misuse of advanced technologies like AI.

DAY 25

Oruthi Maganai

Mutual Separation

"You were born to One Devaki mother, and on that very night of your birth, you became the son of another mother, Yashoda. You grew up in hiding. The evil Kamsa could not tolerate your existence. Threatened by you, the raging jealousy in his belly scorched him. His negative thoughts led to harmful actions for several. But you voided all his evil attempts.

Oh, Lord! You love your faithful devotees. We come here, begging to be fused with You. Please bless us! We will beat the drum while singing in your praise to your divine Consort. With gratitude, we will remember the infinite ways you protect us. We will praise your abundance. We will sing about your valor. This way, our sorrows of separating from you will end, and we will rejoice together."

P*O*E*M Exercise

P (Poetry):

The poet highlights the theme of separation with this verse. In the backstory, Lord Krishna was separated from his birth mother to hide his identity from the evil Kamsa. Raised with love by his foster parents, Krishna grew up to vanquish the malevolent

Kamsa. The devotees have come to unite with Him. They come to fuse with the dharmic qualities and come in gratitude. They wish to laud the valor and hope to end the pain of mutual separation.

O (Observation):

On the face of it, this verse is a simple story. Yet, there are strands of pain in separation. Even Lord Krishna had to experience separation from his parents at birth. Separation from hostile forces outside and within us is another idea strand. Separation for the devotees from the Divine is another suffering. The poet implies adopting divine ways of living and separating adharma from one's life to unite with the One. Very subtly, there is a shift that the Divine must also be united in love.

E (Engagement):

To access the divine, one must adopt the dharma way of living. There is the pain of living when one is tied to evil ways, hence it is a quest to root out the rot within and beyond. We sabotage true happiness by working against the natural law of dharma. It sounds like a moral lecture, but it is not. For example, a simple act of overconsumption comes with a cost for forests, natural resources, the environment, health, and well-being. This is just an example. There may not be any evil intent behind our overconsumption. We may be separated by dharma which advocates critical thought, wisdom, and discrimination. If something is inevitable, we can choose less packaging, purchase alternate products, prevent wasteful consumption, donate, barter, or recycle. We could use knowledge to propel a higher goal. Knowledge and wisdom growth is dharmic.

We could train ourselves to quell the occasional hostility within to become better versions of who we are. Cultivating charity to others is dharma to self and others. Using wisdom is dharma, and so is standing up against bullies. It is dharma to recognize gifts in self and others, be grateful for them, and spread love. These are some examples of the dharmic way of getting close to the One.

The drums they request help spread this loving essence common to many cultures, although they call it dharma in the poet's land.

These are only some examples of the righteous way of getting close to the One. There is a discomfort with the detachment from dharma.

In the modern setting, consider the case of a corporate executive who, driven by intense competition and the pressure to meet financial targets, decides to manipulate financial reports to present a more favorable picture of the company's performance. This compromise in ethical conduct, straying from the principles of honesty and transparency, leads to a short-term boost in stock prices and the executive's personal gains. However, when the truth is eventually revealed, the company faces a significant financial downturn, shareholders suffer losses, employees lose jobs, and the executive's reputation is tarnished. The misery caused by this ethical breach illustrates the pain of separation from divinity, as adherence to dharma would have prioritized honesty and integrity, fostering long-term success, and well-being for all stakeholders.

The story serves as a reminder that compromises in dharma can have far-reaching societal consequences, emphasizing the importance of upholding ethical principles for the well-being of individuals and communities.

Finally, there is the theme of reuniting in this verse. Is there a need for the One to be fused with devotees? This may be a gigantic leap of thought, but *does the Supreme also experience separation pain?*

M (Movement):

The perspective of inseparability from the Divine reflects the power of cultivating gratitude in both good and challenging times. Instead of succumbing to complaints and stress when faced with multiple problems, acknowledging the blessings of having a home, income, vehicle, and good health can bring about a positive shift.

The idea of daily gratitude exercises is a proactive approach to appreciation of life's blessings. Additionally, seeking divine grace during both joys and difficulties reinforces a sense of strength and resilience, turning problem-solving into a celebration of success.

Instead of resorting to substances like alcohol or drugs to numb emotional pain, some individuals find solace, and completeness within themselves through a transformative spiritual connection. Steeping life in the dye of accessible divinity offers an alternative to the sense of separation. Practices like mindfulness, prayer, creative expression, and cultivating a sense of purpose become healthier and more fulfilling ways to address life's challenges and emotional voids. This approach speaks to the potential of finding inner solace and completeness through an active and purposeful spiritual journey.

DAY 26

Male Manivanna!

Perpetual Celebration

"O Beloved, the one with the brilliant sapphire hue! Through this holy month of Margazhi, we perform the penance our elders have done earlier in a sincere manner. This was the only way we knew to get close to you.

"You ask us what we desire. We would like milky-white conches just like the Panchajanyam you blow. When these are blown, the universe should resound, and reverberate with your greatness.

We request enormous drums that vibrate your name and a multitude of devoted singers praying for your perpetuity. In addition, we need bright oil lamps to illumine, flags to show unity with you, and an enormous canopy to celebrate our unison with you.

O Supreme Lord, you are the baby on a banyan leaf. Grace us with your divine presence as we complete the celebration singing your praise."

P*O*E*M Exercise

P (Poetry): In the metaphorical sense, the journey of these girls unfolds into celebration. Once viewing life as an ordinary pebble, they now discover divinity in the daily. Incorporating the soul spirit into their lives, they witness the sparkle, facets, depth, and brilliance that elevate the seemingly mundane. Fusing with the sapphire-hued divine brings a joy that the young maidens cannot keep to themselves. They feel the need to resound and reverberate with this knowledge and fervently pray for this perpetual union. They request gifts for collective well-being.

Viewing the Supreme as a baby on a banyan leaf brings a sense of approachability hitherto unknown.

O (Observation): In the prior verse, the sharp pain of separation gave way to the joy of union, celebrated, shared, and prayed for perpetuity. The requested objects are not for selfish ends but for collective benefit. Bright lamps illumine the darkest corners of our psyche and milky-white conches replace negative output with an outpouring of divinity. Drumbeats resound with positive vibrations, flags and festoons manifest a kindred spirit even in differences, and the canopy provides divine security from negative forces.

No person is too little to contribute, to enjoy, to share divinity. The Supreme lies in *yoga nidra* on the flood waters or *pralaya* in the form of a baby on the banyan leaf. This is a powerful metaphor of the divine manifestation as a baby promoting the idea that no one is lowly while seeking out magnificence.

E (Engagement):

In real-life scenarios, witness the transformative power of incorporating divinity into our daily lives, fostering joy, unity, and collective well-being.

Recognizing Blessings: Embracing divinity encourages us to recognize and appreciate the blessings that often go unnoticed. Take, for instance, a daily gratitude practice where individuals intentionally reflect on the positive aspects of their lives. By acknowledging the seemingly small blessings like the warmth of sunlight or the kindness of a stranger, individuals cultivate a deeper sense of gratitude and contentment.

Holding Life Like a Pebble or a Sapphire

The metaphor of holding life like a pebble or a brilliant sapphire teaches us to appreciate the depth and brilliance within the seemingly ordinary. Consider a community art project where individuals collectively paint and decorate ordinary pebbles, turning them into vibrant, symbolically rich creations. This activity not only transforms the perception of the mundane but also serves as a reminder that every aspect of life, much like a brilliant sapphire, holds potential beauty and significance.

Beyond this art project, there's an invitation to explore the profound essence of a pebble on a more personal level. Just holding a pebble and contemplating its journey adds another layer to this metaphor. Imagine how it came to be, the smoothness earned through tumbling in streams, creating sand, softening edges, and gracefully moving with the flow of nature. Engage with it using all senses, feel its texture with your fingertips, warm it with your hands, and perhaps, consider using it for a hot stone massage. This intimate interaction brings mindful awareness, transforming the perception of a mere pebble into a rich symbol of life's intricate journey. It's a reminder that even the seemingly insignificant elements carry a story, beauty, and significance worth exploring. By infusing these practices into our daily routines, we elevate our understanding of life, recognizing its brilliance and holding each moment with a newfound appreciation.

M (Movement): In our daily lives, incorporating the lessons from Andal and the metaphorical journey of the girls can have profound effects, bringing joy, unity, and a sense of collective well-being.

Collective Well-being in Action: Consider a community initiative where individuals come together to create a shared space for meditation and reflection. Just like the girls' request for bright oil lamps, this space could be adorned with soft lighting to illuminate both physical and metaphorical dark corners. It becomes a collective effort, promoting a sense of unity and well-being for all involved.

Resounding Positivity: Imagine a workplace where employees collectively choose to replace negative conversations with positive affirmations. Much like the milky-white conches replacing negative output by singing about the divine, this practice can create a resounding atmosphere of positivity, fostering a healthier and more supportive work environment.

Unity: In a diverse community or organization, symbolic flags and festoons can represent different cultures and backgrounds. These visual elements can manifest a kindred spirit even in differences, promoting understanding, respect, and unity among the members, not as tribes, but as human beings.

Divine Security in Challenging Times: During challenging times, a community or family could create a symbolic canopy, representing a collective shelter against difficulties. This could take the form of a support group, where individuals come together to share their challenges, providing a sense of help, security, and understanding.

Embracing the Divine Essence

In real-life scenarios, the profound truth that "one is not too small to be divine" unfolds, exemplifying the significance of every individual in holding the fabric of existence. Likewise, no act of kindness is too small.

Celebrating Individual Significance: In a community or workplace project, each person contributes, mirroring that no one is too small to be divine. Every individual's contribution maintains balance within the larger context.

Empowering Children in Education: Implement educational programs that emphasize the unique qualities and contributions of each student. By fostering an environment where every child feels valued, the concept of being divine, regardless of size or age, is instilled from an early age. This empowerment echoes the idea that, like the baby on the banyan leaf, every individual has the potential to hold back overwhelming challenges.

By embodying these practices, we reinforce the understanding that everyone, irrespective of their perceived size or significance, possesses a divine essence that can make a meaningful impact on the collective well-being of the community or society. This verse is both a mindset calibration and a collective celebration.

Movement

The narrator often needs reminders to stick to the path of righteousness. It is hard, but it is the key to survival. Things may go wrong on a specific day for many of us. One can choose to sulk in inaction, curse life, blame others, or expect someone else to solve problems in an unrighteous way. These are reactions that come from being separated from daily divinity. The other option is acting positively to remedy that. One could assess the gifts in life while looking to solve the problem. In that process, one recognizes all blessings, including humanity willing to help if reached out to with humility. The pain of the problem is separated when incorporating righteous solutions. There are people in this world who choose to solve problems through alcohol, drugs, and medications. There may be a void they constantly try to fill with dissatisfaction. Yet, if they gave a chance to steep this fabric of living in the dye of accessible divinity, they might not endure separation anxiety.

DAY 27

Koodarai Vellum

Unison

"You win over enemies, Oh Govinda! We seek only you as the highest reward, and that's why we are here to laud with drums to celebrate with you. By doing so, we will obtain from your gifts of the highest order; presents that are praised by the entire world. First, we will wear the bracelet, the shoulder ornament, the earrings, and their hanging accessories. Then, we will don the anklets, and other beautiful decorations, dressing in beautiful clothes. After that, we will celebrate with rich milk and the sweetest rice. The buttery richness will spill and drip beyond our elbows.

Always stay united with us in this feast where we blissfully wear your gifts and partake in your abundance."

P*O*E*M Exercise

This beautiful verse emphasizes the celebration of the inclusive Divine through a rich and symbolic description of adorning oneself with gifts and partaking in abundance. The celebration involves not just external rituals but an internal transformation and connection with the divine qualities.

P (Poetry Analysis):

Spiritual Embodiment: The verse paints a picture of spiritual richness, starting from wearing divine accessories like bracelets, shoulder ornaments, and earrings. These items symbolize qualities such as strength, support, and attentiveness that devotees seek to embody.

Step by Step Journey: The step by step process, from adorning oneself to celebrating with rich milk and sweet rice, signifies a gradual progression towards spiritual fulfillment. It echoes the idea that spiritual growth is a journey, not a destination.

Sensory Imagery: The description of buttery richness spilling beyond elbows provides a sensory and visual image of abundance. It conveys the idea that the divine celebration is not only internal but also manifests externally, enriching one's entire being.

"The One who Wins over Enemies," another name ascribed to the Supreme, demonstrates the inclusiveness extended to once hostile foes now steeped in dharma.

O (Observation): The observation revolves around the concept of celebration to unite with the divine. It emphasizes the integration of spiritual practices into daily life. The act of wearing divine gifts and celebrating with abundance signifies a conscious effort to align oneself with divine qualities.

E (Engagement): The extension delves into the powerful impact of incorporating divine qualities into daily life. It suggests that living in harmony with the world and embracing dharma leads to a prosperous and blissful life. The examples provided, such as a leader benefiting the team without ego, highlight the transformative potential of adopting divine virtues.

M (Movement): The movement reflects a personal commitment to spiritual well-being. It involves clearing mental cobwebs, paying attention to the body, and focusing on the divine. The practice of respecting others without ego is seen to attract love and reciprocity, aligning with the divine principle of selfless service.

True celebration, according to the narrator, is an infusion of gratitude. Opportunities to celebrate can be small or grand, and even sincere efforts that fail are reasons to celebrate. The reference to the effulgent Spirit serving devotees highlights that events without ego constitute a true celebration. The experiment of dealing with situations with genuine humility is seen to build greater trust, bonds, and reciprocity.

In summary, the verse encourages a holistic celebration of abundance, emphasizing the gradual journey towards fulfillment, and the transformative impact of embodying divine virtues in daily life.

DAY 28

Karavaigal Pinnsendru

Sans Artifice

"O Lord, we are simple folk who know nothing other than following our grazing cows in the forest to feed ourselves.

We are ignorant in the enlightened views of understanding the infinite facets of your supreme nature. What we cowherds know is simply to leverage the blessing of sharing kinship by birth. By this, we're forever linked to you. O Flawless One, Leader of Cowherds!

(Govinda!) We will never ever allow this relationship between us to be swept away.

Out of familiarity with you, we've played and loved you like one of us. We have, in our ignorance, overlooked your greatness, and addressed you in the singular. Please forgive us, and do not mistake this purest love for disrespect.

O Lord and Master! We ask for the divine word of acceptance of our surrender to you."

P*O*E*M Exercise

The profound simplicity and humility expressed in this verse create a touching portrayal of the devotees' relationship with the Supreme. The microcosmic relationship of the cowherd kin stretches to include all creatures as divine kin. The girls fervently wish to hold to divine kinship over baser ties.

P (Poetry):

The poet's perspective of trusting simplicity is in the metaphor of the Supreme Being the Master Cowherd, the keeper of willing souls.

- **Trust and Surrender:** The devotees approach the Supreme with a trusting and surrendering heart. Their simplicity is reflected in their acknowledgment of ignorance about the intricate facets of the Divine. They choose to rely on the blessing of kinship by birth, a relationship they want to preserve and cherish.
- **Familiarity and Forgiveness:** The poet beautifully captures the essence of familiarity and accessibility to the Divine. The devotees have played and loved the Supreme like one of them, addressing Him in the

singular. There's a genuine, unassuming quality to their relationship. The plea for forgiveness emphasizes the humility of the devotees, acknowledging the potential oversight in recognizing the greatness of the Divine.

- **Yearning for Connection:** The verse conveys a deep yearning for a spiritual connection. The devotees seek the "divine word of acceptance" of their surrender. It's beyond complex rituals or scholarly knowledge; it's about the purity of their love and trust, expressed through surrender.

O (Observation):

- **Paradox of the Supreme:** The poem highlights the paradoxical nature of the Supreme, who is both the great Narayana and the accessible Krishna. The devotees grapple with this dichotomy, realizing the simultaneous grandeur, and approachability of the Divine. This observation speaks to the multifaceted nature of the spiritual journey.

- **Simplicity in Devotion:** The simplicity of the devotees becomes a profound aspect of their devotion. Their lack of scholarly knowledge is not a hindrance; instead, it enhances the purity of their love. This simplicity serves as a reminder that the path to the Divine is open to all, regardless of intellectual prowess.

- **Full Circle:** The girls' journey comes full circle as they addressed the Supreme as Narayana in the first verse without realizing His infinitude. Initially perceiving Him as somewhat unreachable, they now address Him with familiarity, considering Him as their own cowherd relative in this verse. While intermittently grasping the magnitude of His divinity, they apologize for being too familiar, realizing that He remains the magnificent Narayana. This newfound familiarity comes because of their own radiance of divinity.

E (Engagement):

In a bustling city, Paro grapples with the relentless pace of individualistic societies eroding her spiritual roots. Despite her stellar academic qualifications, she feels a huge dissatisfaction. Determined to navigate life's uncertainties, she weaves spirituality and kinship to pull the divine into her daily existence, integrating dharmic qualities as a compass. Paro's journey unfolds as kindness becomes her armor, compassion her strength, and discernment her guide.

However, with each perceived success or failure, challenges abound as individualistic currents threaten to pull Paro away from her spiritual center. The struggle to embody these principles is constant, acknowledging the ongoing journey toward self-awareness. Paro's story is a testament to finding strength through spirituality, inspiring seekers to navigate unique paths while celebrating the collective pursuit of the divine amid life's complexities.

- **Paths to the Divine:** The extension explores various paths to understanding the Divine. While knowledge and right action are acknowledged, the verse emphasizes that without the essence of devotion (Bhakti), these paths lose their significance. It underscores the idea that spiritual wisdom and scholarly knowledge, while valuable, must be infused with devotion and love for a holistic understanding of the Divine.

- **Complexity of Understanding:** The verse is a poignant plea for understanding the complexity of the Supreme. It acknowledges that even with devotion, the vastness of the Divine remains a mystery. The struggle to comprehend this paradox is a universal aspect of the spiritual journey.

M (Movement):

Spirituality in Daily Life: The movement reflects on the integration of divine qualities into daily life. It emphasizes the need for a solid core and spiritual roots to navigate life's uncertainties. The challenges of maintaining spirituality in individualistic societies are highlighted, pointing to the importance of exploring the interplay between the individual self and the universal Self.

Strength through Spirituality: The narrative underscores the transformative power of spirituality, leading to qualities such as kindness, compassion, and discernment. The constant struggle to embody spiritual principles is acknowledged, emphasizing the ongoing journey toward self-awareness and consciousness.

This verse beautifully encapsulates the simplicity, humility, and profound depth of the devotees' relationship with the Supreme. It encourages spiritual seekers to embrace the authenticity of their individual paths, fostering a sense of unity and celebration in their collective pursuit of the divine.

DAY 29

Sitram Sirukkale

The Dawning

Oh, Govinda! In the cold wee morning hours, we come here to you only to worship you at your golden lotus-like feet. You're Govinda, born into the community of innocent cowherds. For that kinship alone, you cannot abandon us. So, allow us to serve you in devotion. All we ask of you is to accept our humble offerings.

Look here; you understand everything. Yet why don't you get this simple fact? We seek your grace or word (parai) for today and for generations perpetually. You alone can erase any attachment to material possessions. Our sole aim is to worship you, to be led by you. We want to stay united with you for posterity."

P*O*E*M Exercise

As the devoted girls get closer to completing their vow, the poems get layered, and imbued with an understanding of a mightier force. The extension explores the notion that everyone is "hardwired" to contribute a unique and divine element to daily life. By embracing practices that foster spiritual growth, individuals can tap into their inherent capacity for greatness. This aligns with the idea that the journey toward self-awareness and consciousness is universally accessible, transcending barriers imposed by age, status, or education.

P (Poetry):

- **Simplicity and Divinity:** The poet beautifully captures the simplicity of the cowherd lasses and their genuine devotion to Govinda. The accessibility of the Divine is emphasized, portraying Govinda as not only the Supreme Being but also someone born into the innocence of the cowherd community. This simplicity makes the Divine relatable and approachable.

- **Kinship with the Divine:** The poem delves into the concept of kinship between the devotees and Govinda. The idea that this shared bond prevents abandonment is a powerful expression of the intimate connection between the Divine and the worshiper. It reflects the deep understanding that the Divine is not distant but a part of the same community, bound by love.

- **Fervent Request for Grace:** The poet's plea for Govinda's grace and acceptance of humble offerings showcases the devotion and surrender of the cowherd lasses. Their simplicity and humility shine through as they seek Govinda's word for today and generations to come. The desire to erase attachments to material possessions and to be led by the Divine reveals a profound longing for spiritual unity.

O (Observation):

Transition to Radiant Ignorance: The observation notes the transition of the cowherd lasses into a state of radiant ignorance. This phase represents a beautiful paradox where, despite their lack of scholarly knowledge, they win over the Almighty with their loving divinity. They glow with selfless, unconditional devotion in their quest. The poet subtly points out that this state precedes the union with the Divine.

E (Engagement):

Cultivating Awareness: Maintaining spiritual awareness is akin to nurturing a garden. Just as weeds can grow and threaten the beauty of the garden, negative thoughts, and actions can threaten our spiritual connection. Regular introspection helps in identifying and uprooting these metaphorical weeds.

- **Gratitude for Opportunities:** Every day offers an opportunity for spiritual growth. The sunrise brings a new beginning, a chance to align with the divine. Acknowledging these opportunities and expressing gratitude for them reinforces the connection with the higher self.

- **Practice of Forgiveness:** Forgiveness is a powerful tool on the spiritual journey. It not only mends relationships with others but also cleanses the soul. Just as the cowherd lasses seek forgiveness for their unintentional lapses, we too must forgive ourselves and others, fostering a compassionate heart.

- **Embracing Imperfections:** The cowherd lasses acknowledge their simplicity and ignorance. Similarly, embracing our imperfections, and limitations allows for authentic growth. It's a reminder that the divine connection is not contingent on perfection but on sincerity and effort.

- **Surrendering to the Divine:** The girls express their desire to stay united with the Supreme for posterity. Surrendering to the divine involves relinquishing the ego and trusting in a higher plan. This surrender is not an act of defeat but a conscious choice to be guided by divine wisdom.

- **Integration of Divinity into Daily Life:** The essence of spirituality lies in seamlessly integrating it into daily life. From the wee morning hours to the course of the day, each moment becomes an opportunity to express devotion, gratitude, service, and humility.
- **Living in Posterity:** In this verse, the girls seek continuity in their connection with Govinda for future generations. Similarly, the impact of a spiritual journey is not confined to the individual; it reverberates through time, influencing descendants, and communities positively. The poetry of Andal has withstood time and tide, as this need for spiritual connection is always present.

The spiritual journey involves a continuous loop of introspection, gratitude, empathy, forgiveness, acceptance, surrender, and integration through positive action. It's a dance with the divine, where each step brings us closer to the golden lotus-like feet of Govinda, symbolizing the culmination of the soul's journey in eternal unity. Recognizing the divine in both challenges and joys becomes a transformative and empowering aspect of daily life, contributing to the fulfillment of the soul's hunger for spiritual connection.

M (Movement):

Cultivating Spiritual Courage

As an author, seeking guidance and connection from the Divine in personal life requires courage and the development of a mindset grounded in openness, humility, and trust. Here are practical steps to integrate this courage into daily life:

1. **Create Sacred Moments:**

   - Designate a brief period during the day for quiet reflection and connection with the divine, perhaps in the garden among flowers and herbs.
   - Establish a sacred space or ritual, such as lighting a candle, to transition into a mindset of receptivity, dispelling ignorance, and illuminating the spirit.

2. **Express Gratitude:**

   - Begin and end each day by expressing gratitude for life's blessings.
   - Acknowledge the guidance and support believed to be received from the divine.
   - Practice acts of kindness, both to self, and others.

3. **Mindful Awareness:**

   - Cultivate mindfulness throughout the day, paying attention to thoughts, and actions.
   - Utilize moments of stillness amid a busy day to connect with the divine.

4. **Ask with Sincerity:**

   - Approach the divine with sincerity in the heart, sharing struggles, doubts, and joys.
   - Formulate requests or questions that genuinely reflect one's needs and desires.

5. **Keep a Spiritual Journal:**

   - Maintain a journal to record thoughts, prayers, and reflections.

- Review journal entries to gain insights into one's spiritual journey and responses received.

6. **Practice Gracious Acceptance:**

- Be open to receiving guidance or answers in unexpected ways.
- Trust that the divine communicates through various channels, including intuition, signs, or the wisdom of others.

7. **Reflect on Challenges:**

- When facing challenges, take a moment to seek inner guidance.
- Ask for strength, wisdom, and clarity to navigate difficulties with resilience. It takes humility to request help from the universe, especially for highly independent people.
- Go back to assessing abundance instead of scarcity, the blessings to help solve the challenge.
- Practice charity especially when it is most needed for self, for there are people with bigger challenges.

8. **Participate in Spiritual Community:**

- Engage with a community that shares similar spiritual values.
- Group practices, rituals, or discussions can deepen your connection and provide a supportive environment.

9. **Develop a Mantra or Affirmation:**

- Create a personal mantra or affirmation resonating with your spiritual aspirations.

- Repeat it regularly, especially during moments of uncertainty or when seeking divine guidance.

10. Celebrate Spiritual Milestones:

- Acknowledge and celebrate moments of spiritual growth or insight.
- Recognize the divine presence during times of joy and achievement.

11. Propel Towards Positive Action:

- Choose actions aligned with higher principles, employing proactive constructive approaches.
- Reach out to the world. We are united by shared happiness, the pursuit of joy, and freedom from suffering. Give back to the ones who could benefit from generosity.
- Take care of the giving earth.
- Love yourself and others.
- At the minimum, do not inflict harm on others.
- Recognize the capability to help others, fostering a broader perspective on personal challenges.

12. Practice Forgiveness:

- Use forgiveness as a tool to realign with the spiritual path.

13. Incorporate Fearlessness

- Believe in self and what one puts out in the universe. Trust in that higher power. Be brave while learning something outside your comfort zone, appreciating failure, fighting the good fight, and being fearless of fear itself. Dare to dream, grow the imagination, and extend to rekindle the spark in those who have lost it.

14. Learn and Grow:

- Invest time in learning about different spiritual traditions, practices, or philosophies.
- Invest time in creating more and consuming less. Share these creations.
- Expand understanding of the divine and its manifestations in various aspects of life.

Embracing spiritual courage involves vulnerability, trust in the process, and recognition of the divine in both extraordinary and ordinary aspects of life. Integrating these practices naturally empowers the individual on their journey, making life enjoyable despite challenges. The divine is found in lofty qualities transcending the base ones, thereby encouraging a connection with the innermost highest spirit.

DAY 30

Vanga Kadal

The Word

"We praise Madhava, the One who keeps Lakshmi close to his heart. He churned the ocean of milk for the ambrosia. He is also known as Keshava and Krishna.

The girls have completed the vow. The splendor of divinity is manifested in the luminosity of their moon-like faces. They prayed, worshiped, and vowed to the Lord in Brindavan for that desired Parai (drum, word, submission). The magnificent story of attaining the Parai is dedicated as verses by the daughter of Bhattarpiran, who always dons the tulasi bead and lotus necklace.

The awe-inspiring Lord stands tall with broad shoulders that resemble mountains. With magnetic red eyes and a sacred visage, He's majestic to behold. When these 30 Tamil verses are sincerely understood and recited by devotees, they will receive the benevolent grace and eternal bliss."

P*O*E*M Exercise

P (Poetry): The poet Andal acknowledges the transformative journey of the devotees, expressing that their faces now radiate divinity and bliss, mirroring the divine One. The praise for the Supreme is accompanied by gratitude for the poet's father, who played a crucial role in kindling divinity within her. In a spirit of reciprocity, the poet dedicates the verses to help others realize the divinity within themselves.

O (Observation): The poet's acknowledgment of her father as a guru signifies the importance of guidance in the spiritual journey. The act of sharing these verses is a selfless effort to guide others toward a deeper connection with divinity. The observation here is about recognizing the interconnectedness of all beings and the responsibility to share spiritual wisdom.

E (Engagement): The extension of this journey is reflected in the discipline of dharma, where the devotees actively engage in service, love, and effort. The alignment with dharma and devotion leads to the divine making its presence known to them. This extension emphasizes that spiritual growth is a dynamic process involving actions aligned with higher principles.

M (Movement):

Andal involves a transition from the microcosm of personal understanding to a broader perspective of the Supreme. Although she uses the simple ritual of the bridal vow, she exposes the grandeur of divinity in the daily. Rituals and religions are seen as initial scaffolds or doorways to spirituality, with the recognition that the spiritual path is transcendental.

The author of this book expresses a sincere dedication that revolves around connecting with the vast universe and encouraging readers to delve into the selfless nature of spiritual wisdom. In a manner reminiscent of Andal expressing gratitude to her father for igniting her divinity, she extends heartfelt thanks to her mother for patiently answering her spiritual inquiries. Though a mere speck in the universe, she leaned into her inner goddess to bring forth this book with confident humility. The author is mindful that her interpretation is not perfect, and it may even irk the purist. Like the simple cowherd lasses, she too hopes this offering stands as a sincere voice aiming to propel positivity.

Just as the profound wisdom of spiritual seekers transcends geographical and cultural boundaries, the journey towards our own inner divinity is a perpetual endeavor. Much like cultivating a garden that demands constant care and attention like Vishnu Chitta, our spiritual growth flourishes when nurtured with sincerity and humility. The essence of divinity, akin to loftiness, risks fading amidst the challenges of life's complexities. Yet, as we traverse the path of self-discovery, let us remember that our commitment to positive action and continuous tending will guide us towards the enduring light of higher consciousness to unlock infinite opportunities. Through sincere exploration and shared reflections, may we collectively illuminate the way for ourselves and others, fostering a world enriched by the timeless truths that unite diverse spiritual traditions.

Acknowledgment

Andal's poetic devotion breathed life into every word, infusing this book with a timeless grace that simply wouldn't exist without her influence. My heartfelt gratitude extends to this revered poet for her profound impact.

To my beloved circle of family and friends, your gentle nudges and unwavering support served as the driving force behind the completion of this book. Captain G.R.Gopinath, thank you for the foreword and your eloquent perspective. Thank you Vishnuprabha for patiently going through several iterations to capture the vision of the book cover. I would like to thank Shiri, Achuta, and Akila for encouraging, inspiring, and believing in me.

It is my sincerest hope that this work marks a new beginning, and for that, I am eternally grateful.

Glossary

1. Alwars – Tamil saints who espoused devotion through poetry
2. Atasi – Flax flower
3. Dhanur – The auspicious month before harvest also known as Margazhi or Mrigasheera
4. Ikshana – Beholding the Supreme in the entirety
5. Kadamba – Bur flower
6. Kanakambara – A tropical flame flower, its literal translation is golden sky
7. Margazhi Dhanur or Mrugasheera month
8. Napinnai Goddess – Consort of Vishnu
9. Notru Chuvargam
10. Ongiulagalantha
11. Panchajanyam – Vishnu's conch
12. Panchashayanam – Luxurious cotton mattress
13. Parijata – Fragrant night or coral jasmine
14. Parai Drum, promise, word, Nonesuch; Parai is a polysemic word
15. Pasuram Alwar composed poems
16. Pavai Nonbu – The bridal vow of the damsels
17. Periya Piratti – The goddess Mahalakshmi
18. Pirantha Maaya – The Master Magician who takes birth in a human form while hiding the greatness.
19. Poo-chendu – Flower posy shaped like a ball

20. Prajña Chakshu – The conscious, intuitive eye
21. Samayapathi – The Lord equal to Devotee
22. Saulabhya – The approachable quality the Supreme adopts to get closer and not overpower devotees.
23. Siru-Parai – Small drum
24. Tiruppavai – Thirty poems or pasurams in praise of the Supreme attributed to Andal
25. Tulasi – Holy basil
26. Valampuri – Sacred conch shell. When blown, the sound creates positive vibrations leading to prosperity.
27. Valiya – Chirping birds
28. Vishwaroopam – Universal Form and the Form of the Universe
29. Yoga Nidra – Conscious Sleep
30. Pippala tree – Sacred fig
31. Visishtadvaita – A philosophy of qualified dualism that holds the view that all diversity ultimately stems from a fundamental underlying unity.
32. Tulabharam – The act of offering the Supreme material gifts by weighing self on one scale and putting items of value on the other scale until the weight is equal on both sides of scale. It is more a devotee belief in the hope of giving back.